MOM'S TRAPPED in the MINIVAN

Surviving Your Child's Middle Years
with Your Sanity *and Salvation* Intact!

CYNTHIA SUMNER

BARBOUR
PUBLISHING

The author is represented by Alive Communications, Inc., 7680 Goddard Street, Suite 200, Colorado Springs, CO 80920.

Published by Barbour Publishing, Inc., P.O. Box 719, Uhrichsville, Ohio 44683, www.barbourbooks.com

Our mission is to publish and distribute inspirational products offering exceptional value and biblical encouragement to the masses.

 Member of the
Evangelical Christian
Publishers Association

Printed in the United States of America.
5 4 3 2 1

To all of my friends who keep

helping me become a better mom

and a better person.

I am eternally grateful.

Acknowledgments

Without the contributions of so many helpful souls, this book wouldn't have made it out of the minivan. A big thanks goes to—

my husband, John, who has never shirked his share of housework and has gone above and beyond the call of duty during my deadline;

my children, Spencer, Shelby, and Ross, who make life so very interesting and keep me on my toes;

my parents, Van and Be Wolford, who travel thousands of miles each year to give me a break and help keep my sanity intact;

my friends, Tina Acree, Anne Zumwalt, Deanna Lustfeldt, Kathy Orme, Cheryl Geiger, Teri Edris, and Lisa Oster, who took time out of their own busy schedules to share their stories and laugh, a lot;

my agent, Chip MacGregor, who continues to guide my career with wisdom and patience;

my editor, Shannon Hill, who put up with a roller coaster of a year from me and hung on for the ride.

Contents

Introduction

Say what you like. It's not cool. It's not hip. It's definitely not sexy, but I love my eight-year-old minivan. It is my home away from home these days—each passing year marked by a specific dent, scratch, or carpet stain. Arriving the same year as our third and youngest child, it's been the mode of transportation for our annual cross-country car trip vacations. More importantly, my minivan operates on a daily basis as a school bus and kiddy limousine for our children and their assorted friends, as a motorized office, Barcalounger, and as a window on the world for me.

In this mobile season of life, I've learned that it's possible to do just about anything in a vehicle. Forget about the ordinary, albeit unsafe, activities most of us undertake while driving one-handed—like eating, applying makeup, or talking on the cell phone. We are multitaskers after all! I can also read, write, help a child with homework, catch up on current events, give myself a manicure, and even sleep once I've parked the car to wait for the emergence of my child from an activity—and oh, how many activities there are these days.

During my children's early years, I so looked forward to the time when we would outgrow all their schedules: sleeping schedules, feeding schedules, potty schedules, medication schedules. However, I ended up just substituting those schedules for others, which usually are written on the calendar in three different colors, one for each of our three kids. (My husband's and my engagements are recorded in less obtrusive black.)

Of course, most of these scheduled activities occur someplace other than our home, which means one thing: *We be driving.* Here's a simple riddle. How do you know you're spending too much time in the car? Answer: when most of your interactions with other mothers are limited to waving as you pass on the road. What's scary about this is that I can identify my friends' vehicles before getting close enough to see their faces!

Dare I say that all this driving and parking and sitting often feels like a waste of time? My head reminds me of the importance of enriching our children's lives through exposure to music, sports, and intellectual pursuits, especially since we live in a small, sheltered farming community. But a funny thing happened on the way to all the classes, studios, and gymnasiums. My heart began to yearn nostalgically for those long days at home when we focused more on each other and less on the mystery location in which the latest uniform or piece of equipment had disappeared.

And my spirit? Instead of considering peace-building faith, it wallows in thoughts of my own mortality each time my head remembers that most accidents occur within ten miles of home. Given this fact, it's difficult to know whether to rejoice or to complain that less than half of our trips fall within that radius— by necessity most are considerably longer. Fortunately, the majority of our driving is along backcountry roads, but on those occasions when we travel into the "city," I certainly feel it is *"not safe to travel about."* Other drivers do seem to be in turmoil wherever we go, perhaps from being in as much of a hurry and as tired of chauffeuring as I am.

Many times my children and I pray for God's protection while we're on the road—during slippery conditions and low visibility, dense traffic, and road construction. As the wandering tribes of Israel proclaimed in Joshua 24:17, "[God has] protected us on our entire journey and among all the [cities] through which we traveled." Including the time a commuter running late for an appointment knocked us onto the tracks of an oncoming train. Even though our car was rendered undrivable, at least we weren't hit by the train!

Although we usually don't have to contend with rush-hour gridlock, the moms I strike up conversations with while sitting in the parking lot all tell the same story (with a sigh): "After this, I have to take Sara to the dentist, run Justin to Cub Scouts, and stop by the store to pick up something for dinner." If moms question the relevance of their lives while changing poopy diapers and trying to remove crayon art from walls, finding meaning in this season of chauffeurism can be even more difficult.

With so many choices of things to do, moms (especially yours truly) are tempted to set up busyness as an idol, something to be pursued and honored, even at the expense of time spent with our Lord and our families. We tend to encourage that same level of activity in our children, as well. Why do I feel I need permission to slow down the pace? God desires that we rest: "At your rebuke, O God of Jacob, both horse and chariot lie still" (Psalm 76:6). There are days when I long for someone, anyone, to tell me, "No rushing around today. Your chariot (a.k.a. the Dodge Caravan) is not running."

In the modern remake of the classic movie *Sabrina*, the budding photographer remarks, "More isn't always better. Sometimes it's just more." As the middle years begin, you'll find yourself looking down a brand-new road lined with different signposts, detours, and directions—some relating to your child and some for you, too. We may think we follow the most highly rewarded route by playing the "good" mom and running ourselves ragged driving to (and paying for) every activity under the sun available to our kids. The question is, *Who are we really serving while we're trapped in the minivan?*

Sometimes being strong for your children means restricting what they do so there is still time to enjoy each other and take advantage of teachable moments—before kids morph into that alien species called teenagers. A mom also demonstrates strength as often in what she chooses not to do, such as

not performing the majority of the work on your child's school project, even though you know it will turn out better and receive a higher grade

not attending every single sporting event if there is a conflict with something that's very important to you (especially if you have a stand-in available like your husband or a grandparent)

not allowing your child to believe the myth that "you can have it all."

What's the reward of *not* doing things for your family? It's having a morning or evening free to join a Bible study, the opportunity to rediscover friendships with other women, and the time to enjoy open communication and fun with your children (not while in the minivan). What moms need most is to find balance: balance between stillness and activity, between family relationships and the world outside, between staying home and *driving*. Are you feeling trapped by everyone's expectations, including your own?

Perhaps the key to surviving the middle years is to remind yourself that, just like with today's cars, it's not the years you ride through together, it's the mileage you cover that determines your value at trade-in time. The work you do while traveling through the middle years will be rewarded. My hope is that this book will encourage you on your journey. Come on. . .let's make it a road trip!

Roller-Coaster Roles

I've heard the elementary-school phase referred to as the "golden years" of child rearing. You've made it past immersion in your child's bodily fluids, literally and figuratively. You've survived the rebellion of the "terrible twos," something child development experts say won't be revisited until puberty. Your child is dressing independently, eating without assistance, and, hopefully, taking some responsibility for household chores. Add the fact that most kids are now out of the house for long periods, and your days do seem to shine with the promise of something golden: free time. My problem is, I have yet to hit the mother lode!

Much to my surprise, my kids did not automatically become self-sufficient little individuals simply because they entered school. (I know. What was I thinking?) In fact, their behavior and needs reminded me of the ups and downs of a roller coaster, riding the heights of self-confidence one minute and in a steep free fall the next. For instance, at a vacation rest stop, our six-year-old son announced loudly that he would not go into the ladies' rest room—he was going in the men's. I positioned myself at the door only to see him reemerge a minute later because he couldn't unbutton his shorts.

I could almost feel the *click-click-click* as the developmental roller-coaster car crawled upward the day my daughter asserted that it was embarrassing for me to give her a hug or a kiss good-bye around her friends. Still, some evenings, she comes flying back down the other side of the coaster and begs to sit in my lap. Last year our youngest son, who still slept with his blankie, informed me that it was not cool to wear shirts with cute pictures of animals on them. So I sadly gave away the last of the garments decorated with Winnie the Pooh and Tigger, too (except my own, of course).

Obviously, children this age feel conflicted about the level of independence they want to enjoy at different times and in various circumstances. One day they don't want you to walk them up to school; the next they refuse to get out of the car unless you accompany them to the front door of a friend's house. All this vacillating can leave moms feeling frustrated and confused with their kids and with themselves. Even when they are taking two steps forward and one step back, elementary-school children clearly are working hard to become a new creation—to emerge from the cocoon of the preschool years and test their wings.

One mom shared how her daughter expressed excitement about her future role as a mom. On an afternoon when she, her six-year-old daughter, and her mother (Grandma) were eating lunch together and talking about the future, her child commented, "One day I'll be a mom. Mommy, you'll be a grandma, and Grandma, you'll be dead." Talk about getting pushed out of your role prematurely! However, if we're no longer the person whose life is defined by wiping noses and bottoms, who exactly are we? What is our role with regard to our children in the middle years?

In her book *Your Child's Self-Esteem*, Dorothy Corkille Briggs defines the middle years as a "time for developing physical, social, and academic competence. You help with [these skills] when you

- encourage your children to join constructive groups of their age;

- actively support groups they enjoy;

- make your home available to friends;

- avoid giving so many home responsibilities that there's little time for activities with chums; and

- avoid making them feel guilty for cutting the apron strings."[1]

At this stage, you still are the primary role model and

communicator of attitudes and values. A mother's love and affirmation protects her child from the harsh realities of group dynamics, even while her youngster's focus is shifting toward his or her peers.

Ecclesiastes 3:1 states, "There is a time for everything, and a season for every activity under heaven." As children grow, our attention shifts from teaching basic life skills—such as eating, dressing, and using the toilet—to focusing more on details and subtleties. It's like switching from scribbling in a coloring book to staying within the lines. This change in emphasis can make our mothering role feel more like that of taskmaster than teacher or playmate. The first signs of frustration our mellow third child exhibited toward me began with the introduction of homework and piano lessons. Pouting and tears were new behaviors for him, at least when directed toward an adult. Adjusting to my new role was difficult for both of us!

If I had to characterize our children's middle years in terms of a game show, I'd call it *The Waiting Game*. There were the usual daily waits: waiting in line at the store or waiting to talk to a "real live" person on the phone. There was also the customary wait for my children to get ready to go anywhere, as well as a wait for them to return. I felt trapped—first in my home away from home, the minivan, then by the waiting game my life had become. I was even waiting for God to let me know His will for my life.

I am not particularly patient and therefore not all that great at waiting. As the days and miles rolled by, my prayers changed from, "In the morning, O Lord, you hear my voice; in the morning I lay my requests before you and wait in expectation" (Psalm 5:3) to "Free me from the trap that is set for me, for you are my refuge" (Psalm 31:4). I was having trouble coming to terms with the fact that I was starting a new phase of my life, too—along with all that meant.

Spurred on by the desire to take a temporary break from the waiting game and to lay claim to some of that mother lode of free time, I engaged in a quest to rediscover or reinvent myself, to define this new creation. This goal leads to the second real reason I have yet to strike gold: commitments. For those of us who thought we sent our Supermom complex packing along with our children's backpacks and lunch boxes, this season offers brand-new opportunities to extend her another invitation.

Today there are many more people, groups, and organizations in need of volunteers than moms with time available, which means you will be inundated with requests for help at school, church, extracurricular activities, charities, and even in your neighborhood. Erma Bombeck said her youngest child went to school knowing one phrase: "My mom can drive." (You're not the only one who wants to tap in to your "free time" mother lode!) Almost all these volunteer positions offer you the opportunity to do something good, and if your service for the past several years has been limited to cooking, laundry, and housework, it can be hard to turn down such worthwhile endeavors.

I, myself, am guilty of misinterpreting Paul's urging in Ephesians 6:7–8 to "serve wholeheartedly, as if you were serving the Lord, not men, because you know that the Lord will reward everyone for whatever good he does" as an exhortation to serve on any committee that called and asked.

Eventually I realized I was riding a roller coaster of my own making.

> Click. I'll be room mother because it's important to
> be involved at my child's school.
> Click. Our church needs someone to teach Sunday
> school and I love that age group.
> Click. My daughter's Girl Scout troop needs a
> leader or the group will disband.
> Click. The local library needs someone to partici-
> pate on the board of directors.

My car kept climbing to the pinnacle of busyness until I reached the top and went over into the long fall of "too much to do."

I rushed headlong into my idea of what my new role should be without consulting my Creator. "Be still before the Lord and wait patiently for him" (Psalm 37:7). As exasperating as waiting can be, sometimes it serves a purpose. After my first, fairly unsuccessful attempt at making myself into a new creation, I took a step back and embraced the wisdom of this observation: *Between the wish and the thing lies waiting.* There is so much to look forward to during children's middle years, in their lives and in ours. The challenge is finding balance between a mom's independence and the ties that bind us to our families.

How can we smooth out the bumps on the roller coaster of life during the early years? First, moms should recognize that their children need them as intensely as they did in the preschool years. Your role may have changed, the time requirements may have lessened, but kids still require the love, acceptance, and security a mother provides. Try to establish a routine of doing something special with your child—that doesn't include driving her to a weekly lesson or sitting on a bench watching her perform an activity. You both will enjoy the one-on-one time together! If you have trouble prying your child away from her friends, invite them to come along. Introduce yourself to their parents and make getting together a family affair. (This is a good idea at any stage.)

Making changes in your own schedule really helps slow down the daily roller coaster. Often it's easier to switch than fight, so I've become "The Accommodator." For the longest time, I couldn't figure out why I seemed to have less time available with my children in elementary school. Then I realized that, when they were preschoolers, I followed a pattern of doing something with the kids, doing some work, doing something else with the kids, doing some more work, all day long until they went to bed. Now I have to accomplish *everything* between eight in the morning and three in the afternoon because from that point until about nine at night, the minivan and I are at their beck and call. That means housekeeping, errands, grocery shopping, volunteering, and, oh yes, writing need to be basically finished before I pick them up from school. (Okay, it doesn't always work out that way, but I do my best.)

To accommodate my kids' need to have me available in the evenings, I've also changed the timing of the activities I undertake. When they were little, I usually joined groups that met in the evenings when my husband was home from work. Now it's very difficult to fit *my* evening activities in between everyone else's. Again, I'd rather switch my activities to the daytime, when possible, than fight my kids' schedules.

Big changes will rock your child's world—and your world, too—in this new phase of life. In the movie *Parenthood*, the grandmother talks about the feeling of riding a roller coaster as a metaphor for life with children. Fast, exhilarating, scary. Some people prefer riding the merry-go-round, Grandma says, but that didn't do anything for her. It was too safe, too mundane. The ups and downs of the middle years can make you want to scream or make you hold your breath, but just like Grandma, I wouldn't have it any other way.

Mom's Moments

You may have heard the phrase "Don't sweat the small stuff," but as our children grow, so does the "stuff" we have to deal with—in difficulty and importance. Don't underestimate the amount of emotional energy it takes to deal with the larger concerns of the middle years. Build some time to rest into your schedule to recover from the roller-coaster ride.

If you do find yourself with some free time on your hands, don't squander it! Pick up an activity you may have put aside when your children were younger or try out a new interest.

If you feel unsure about what kind of "new creation" God is calling you to become, remember the scriptural promise that "he who began a good work in you will carry it on to completion until the day of Christ Jesus" (Philippians 1:6). Let God lead you into new endeavors.

School Daze

Let my teaching fall like rain and my words descend like dew,
like showers on new grass, like abundant rain on tender plants.

DEUTERONOMY 32:2

Of all the misconceptions I had about life with children, my ideas about schooling may have been farthest from the mark. I thought you just sent your kids off to school each day and they returned in the afternoon brimming with new knowledge and stories about all the fun things they did. Sometimes mine did, but they also came home with homework assignments on things like stem and leaf plots (the new, new math) and stories about fights at recess (complete with injuries as proof). In many ways, surviving having children in the public-school system has been more of a challenge for me than for them.

Undoubtedly some readers are nodding their heads and thinking, *That's why we send our kids to Christian schools*, or *That's why we homeschool*. However, these choices were not options for us. Since we live in a small rural community, the closest Christian school was a prohibitive distance away. As far as homeschooling goes, let's just say I don't have the right temperament for the job—a fact borne out by the difficulties the kids and I have completing lengthy homework assignments from time to time.

So off to public school our children have gone, and my educational focus has changed as a result. Locked doors, conflict resolution lessons, homework in kindergarten, computers in the classroom. Times have changed; it's simply not enough to focus on the three Rs anymore. Now kids need street smarts, technological know-how, and time-management skills—and I'm expected to help teach these to them. As far as primary curricula goes, I remember being divided into reading groups in first grade. "See the red ball." Now, if a child hasn't started reading sight words by the end of kindergarten, parents fear he won't receive the coveted label "gifted." In fact, learning to read is the first educational trial by fire most parents and kids encounter.

Of course, my husband and I expected our first child to be an early reader. We'd laid the groundwork by reading to him from infancy, plus we both are serious book hounds. Early prescreening tests confirmed his advanced vocabulary. Although he acted supremely uninterested in our attempts to have him learn simple words, we were sure that the "shower" of words at school would stimulate his innate interest (which just shows how little we understood the process). First of all, the rate that information is presented to kids at school these days hardly could be described as "abundant rain"—torrential downpour would be more like it! Add to that our own increasingly exasperated reading sessions at home, and our son probably felt bombarded by a hailstorm of words and phonetics.

The truth is, son No. 1 didn't become a good reader until second grade, when something seemed to click and he began poring over everything in sight. (This same child made perfect scores on his standardized tests last year.) You'd think we'd have learned by the time our daughter started school, but she was such a precocious and *verbal* youngster that we were certain she would be an early reader. She, too, caused us much angst by waiting until second grade to truly develop her reading skills. When son No. 2 wasn't reading fluently by the beginning of first grade, my husband and I merely sighed and remarked, "Just like the others."

What have I taken away from these experiences, besides the fact that the English language often seems to have more exceptions than hard-and-fast rules? I've learned that developmental timetables don't cease to exist because my children have entered their elementary-school years. Some developmental psychologists believe that children are not necessarily *biologically* ready to read simply because they've reached their sixth birthdays. That said, there are things you can do at home to encourage your emerging reader throughout the middle years:

- Continue reading regularly both to and with your child. This is not an overused cliché.

In fact, mom and school principal Dr. Lorrie Simington says, "When I look back at my own children, I just wish I would have read to them more."

- For beginning readers, select a familiar book or one with familiar vocabulary.

- As your child is reading, help him by supplying the word when he hesitates or by offering a clue of some kind.

- To overcome "reading resistance," try reading a story to your youngster first, then read it together, or take turns reading alternate pages.

- Keep reading fun by allowing older children to read things like joke books, magazines, or even comic books.

- Encourage your child to write often—writing leads naturally to reading because they reinforce each other.

One marked difference in curriculum from my elementary-school years is how soon and how often kids write. Because of the importance of the reading-writing connection, teachers spend a lot of time having students write about what they read or about their own experiences. Our youngest son's first essay in second grade yielded some surprising insights:

When I was just a baby my dad was chanjing my diper wen I pead in his fase. He cust out loud. I was too liddil to reemimber this but my brother told me this.

I'm not sure who was more embarrassed by this anec-dote, my husband or me. Our feelings of distress increased as his teacher later shared how she had asked the kids to stand up and read the drafts of their essays before the class, an activity she decided to discontinue after hearing our son's story. I've always wondered what it would be like to live with a class clown—looks like I'm going to find out!

Undoubtedly, school offers endless opportunities for kids to demonstrate their individual personalities, interests, and abilities; however, most curricula do not accommodate chil-dren's unique aptitudes. Is it better to use manipulative "counters" to figure out math problems or to fill in several worksheets? Does your child prefer to work in groups or individually? In the book *Frames of Mind,* Dr. Howard Gardner explains his theory of multiple intelligences, which asserts there are at least seven different ways in which people collect and process information.[2] Most of us learn best by employing one or two methods, so you may recognize your child in several of the following descriptions:

Linguistic intelligence. Those who are highly linguistic enjoy reading, writing, telling stories, and playing word games. They learn effectively in the traditional school atmosphere through listening, reading, writ-ing, and discussing.

Logical-mathematical intelligence. This type of intelligence encompasses the three interrelated fields of mathematics, science, and logic. A person with well-developed logical-mathematical intelligence learns through experimentation, asking questions, and doing calculations.

Spatial intelligence. These children think in images and pictures and enjoy doodling, drawing, and painting. They can "visualize" things in different ways or from new perspectives.

Bodily-kinesthetic intelligence. Does your youngster learn best by doing rather than watching or listening? Those with bodily-kinesthetic intelligence like to dance, run, build, and touch things.

Musical intelligence. The musically inclined can be heard singing, whistling, humming, or tapping their feet and hands. They may remember information better when it is put to music (like the "ABC Song").

Interpersonal intelligence. These kids enjoy bouncing ideas off of others. They interact well with people of diverse ages and often excel on a team or with group assignments, playing the role of leader or follower as appropriate.

Intrapersonal intelligence. Does your child ask hard-to-answer questions about the meaning of life? Those with well-developed intrapersonal intelligence are in touch with their inner needs and feelings. They enjoy dreaming, setting goals, and working independently.

Recognize anybody? One of the things I like about the theory of multiple intelligences is the implication that all children are able to learn, *especially* if information is presented in a format that complements their intelligence style. This means that you can help your child with school by training her to study and select projects based on her natural interests and talents. If you are unsure which way of learning best applies to your youngster, watch how she spends her free time. What does she do when she has to choose an activity? (You might have to rule out TV, the computer, video games, and handheld electronics in advance to get a true picture.) Be cognizant of the differences between your preferred learning style and that of your child. For example, my husband cannot understand how our kids can study and actually retain information while listening to the radio—something I've always done, too.

Finding a child's best learning method will help as you wrestle with the demon of students and parents everywhere: homework. Let's face it: Elementary-school material is not rocket science. Any parent who's made it through high school should be able to help with *most* of the concepts kids are learning in the middle years. Sure, there's new terminology to go along with the new math, and the average parent won't have a clue where to find a dangling participle. But why do our kids stubbornly fight us after they ask for our help with homework? "Listen, my son, to your father's instruction and do not forsake your mother's teaching. They will be a garland to grace your head and a chain to adorn your neck" (Proverbs 1:8–9). My mother tells me our children will discover the truth of this proverb for themselves. . . after another ten years. In the meantime, we have struggled mightily to develop homework strategies we can all live with.

According to research, homework helps students in early elementary grades learn to work independently and encourages self-discipline and responsibility. In later elementary years, gradually increasing amounts of homework may actually improve academic achievement. How much is too much? Educators recommend not more than twenty minutes of homework for first through third graders and twenty to forty minutes for fourth- through sixth-grade students. Here are some additional homework tips from education professionals:

Set a regular time. Keep in mind that the best schedule is one that works for both your child and your family.

Pick a good spot. Location isn't really important as long as your child has good lighting, ready access to books and supplies, and peace and quiet.

Keep out distractions. Set a policy of no TV or other loud noise while studying.

I thought you should know what's recommended before I share what happens at our house. We do not have set time for homework—which is to say there is no time after school when everyone collectively sits down to do their assignments.

Our youngest prefers to do his homework right after he gets home, which suits me fine because he needs the most supervision. The oldest child always needed a break from intellectual pursuits before turning his attention to homework; however, our goal was to have all homework done before dinner or shortly thereafter. Any later, and we all tended to suffer from short attention spans and brain drain. There were instances when my oldest son procrastinated on his homework until close to bedtime. I remember sitting at the table, trying to remain calm and encouraging and failing miserably, while he stared off into space and work grinded to a halt. It took only a few of these sessions before he realized that waiting until the last minute was not in his best interest.

All three of our kids found it easiest to do their homework at the kitchen table while in elementary school. From my standpoint, it worked well, too, because I could be available to answer questions while working on dinner or washing the dishes, but I wasn't hovering. My kids were isolated from distractions, and they felt independent but not abandoned.

As the designated homework monitor, one of my biggest questions is how much I should be helping. The safest way to answer is to ask your child's teacher—if you're lucky, the teacher will send home this information when school starts. It may seem like cheating to look over completed assignments. However, we usually look over our kids' homework to make sure they understand the concepts they are studying. With crowded classrooms and so much material to cover, teachers do not always have the time necessary to give your child the individualized attention they may need on difficult topics.

In her book *99 Ways to Get Your Kids to Do Their Homework*

(and Not Hate It), Mary Leonhardt asserts, "Having homework done right isn't nearly as important as having it done independently. Keep saying to yourself, It's *grade school*. Who cares if he gets an A on homework? It's much more important that children learn to handle assignments on their own."[3] I completely agree, except with children as young as second grade receiving letter grades, I worry more about their self-esteem than the fact that I looked over some homework. Kids this age *do* notice whether their performance is "good" or "poor," and elementary school is a little early to be labeled.

So, do we have a perfect homework system at the Sumner house? *No!* My husband says that if we had a dollar for every time our kids wailed, "That's not how we do it in class," we'd have enough saved to send them to college! There's a fine line between acting supportive and being your child's punching bag for intellectual frustration. As with every other skill, your goal should be to help your child work toward independence. One thing we resolved to avoid is caving in and fixing the kids' homework ourselves. I am willing to put on my editor's hat and explain things done incorrectly, but it's up to them to make the changes (painful as that may be for both of us). A struggle over a specific assignment may signal that something's wrong with the assignment or that your student is having a bad day. However, daily arguments about homework can relate to some other difficulty and indicate the need to consult with the school staff.

There are three sets of circumstances when I've communicated with my children's teacher(s): at the regular back-to-school conference, if I felt my child was having social or academic problems in school, and if the teacher called me.

Has anyone else had the pleasure of being called in to meet with the teacher *before* a regularly scheduled conference? Getting that phone call is not a good sign! Parent-teacher meetings at school can be very intimidating, particularly when your kids are in the early elementary years. There's something about sitting across the table from a teacher—in chairs close enough to the floor that your knees are under your chin—that makes you feel three or four feet tall. . .and I generally had good experiences when I attended school! From the beginning, even a regularly scheduled conference experience tends to promote anxiety because the purpose is to let you know what your child is doing well and to provide feedback and constructive criticism on how he or she can improve. If it's any comfort, some of the educators I spoke with find meetings with parents every bit as uncomfortable because so many parents today place the blame for their child's problems squarely on the teacher.

Early in your child's school career, you still may be deluded into thinking your youngster is nearly perfect, so running into the differences between your perception and that of an impartial teacher can be a shock. I had a bit of difficulty believing that my darlings had snapped in frustration at a teacher or convinced an aggressive child to climb into the toy cabinet and shut the door behind him. (I'm sure he didn't realize that the door automatically locked!) Regardless of the tone the teacher takes, the information presented can put a mom on the defensive, which is not the best way to build a consensus. Here are some tried-and-true strategies for a productive school conference:

Before you meet. Put aside any unpleasant memories of your own educational experiences. Get acquainted with teachers early in the school year, before problems arise. We made a point of always scheduling a meeting with the teacher of our child with attention deficit/hyper-activity disorder (ADHD) prior to the start of school to discuss techniques for keeping him on task during class. Don't assume that teachers will communicate with each other from one year to the next. It's wise to present information about your child anew each year. Collect examples of your student's work to discuss. Make a list of questions, and ask your child if there's anything he or she would like to know from the teacher.

During the conference. Try to begin on a positive note by sharing what your child enjoys about class. Approach the discussion with a cooperative spirit. Jointly consider the question, How can we work together to provide the best learning experience and instruction for this child? Try to keep the emphasis on your child and his or her performance without mak-ing comparisons to other children. Ask the teacher about goals for your student and make sure they are compatible with your own. Let the teacher know what's going on at home—any changes in health, family situations, or living arrangements that may affect academic performance. So that you don't spend an excessive amount of time on disagreements, offer suggestions tactfully and ask for guidance. Listen closely to what the teacher has to say, and summarize points of agreement and disagreement before leaving the conference. Together, come up with a plan covering what the teacher will work on in the classroom and how you can help at home.

Following up. With your child, discuss information covered in the conference. Ask him or her for input on the goals that were set, then take advantage of phone calls and notes to keep up with your child's progress throughout the year.

Proverbs 4:7 states, "Wisdom is supreme; therefore get wisdom. Though it cost all you have, get understanding." Conferences offer the opportunity for parents to gain wisdom of their own. It may require some self-restraint, but you will find out how your child behaves when outside your sphere of influence. At a third-grade conference, I discovered the reason our son wasn't participating in classroom discussions. He was sitting at the back of the room and had ten to twenty paperback books crammed into his desk. At least we no longer had to worry about his reading ability!

One of my favorite stories about Jesus as a child refers to His thirst for knowledge. On a trip to Jerusalem to celebrate the Feast of the Passover, Jesus stayed behind after His parents had left for home.

Thinking he was in their company, they traveled on for a day. Then they began looking for him among their relatives and friends. When they did not find him, they

went back to Jerusalem to look for him. After three days
they found him in the temple courts, sitting among the
teachers, listening to them and asking them questions.
Everyone who heard him was amazed at his under-
standing and his answers (Luke 2:44–47).

After Jesus' mother recovered from her fright, she treasured this event in her heart (v. 51). Wouldn't we all love for our children to be so diligent in their pursuit of wisdom?

Throughout our kids' school years, we'll encounter many opportunities to support their spiritual growth and development. In the Bible, Job encourages, "Let us discern for ourselves what is right; let us learn together what is good" (Job 34:4). There are weeks when I spend more time fleshing out the moral and spiritual questions our children bring home than listening to them read or helping with homework, but I consider this work every bit as important.

When we talk together about why Caleb pushed Sara and what we can do to help or why Caitlyn was calling people names, I have the chance to encourage my kids toward kind behavior. They can learn not to condemn others until they have walked in their shoes, that God loves the child who misbehaves, too, and that loving each other is the greatest thing we can do. Our children have to live in the world, so now is the time to use these teachable moments to instill appropriate values. As youngsters become stronger in their understanding of the difference between right and wrong, they act as a light to the others around them.

Sending your children off to school is a scary experience. Moms spend the early years of kids' lives nurturing them like "tender plants," and the prospect of the outside world storming down on them can lead us to respond in fear when youngsters come to us with problems and questions. Remember, you are still learning, too! "God is exalted in his power. Who is a teacher like him?" (Job 36:22). We can take comfort in the fact that God is always ready to provide us with His excellent guidance and instruction.

Mom's Moments

If you have the time to volunteer in your child's classroom, do it! Spending time there gives you unique insight into the workings of the class, as well as the personalities of the other students. You'll be helping a busy teacher, too.

Make a point of asking your children open-ended questions about their day to keep in touch. It may take a little practice to get more descriptive responses than "fine" or "boring."

Continue praying for your children, as well as for teachers, counselors, and administrators. Cheri Fuller writes in Helping Your Child Succeed in Public School, "As our children grow and we gradually lose direct control, we have a vital, important resource to support them and cooperate with God's working in their lives—prayer."[4]

Who's Your Buddy, Who's Your Pal?

If one falls down, his friend can help him up. But pity the man
who falls and has no one to help him up!

ECCLESIASTES 4:10

For those of us control-oriented moms (notice I did not say control *freak*) who used to "facilitate" play dates, the friends our kids choose for themselves during the middle years can be a bit unexpected. Though reasonably well behaved, my children tended to be attracted to other kids with the "bad boy" (or girl) syndrome. One of the first playmates my son invited over was a child with a serious addiction to the World Wrestling Federation. The only wrestling I had ever seen was the Olympic sport, so "body slam" and "pile driving" were not part of my vocabulary. After the boys went a couple of rounds, I had to sit them down and tell our guest that my son enjoyed having him over, but that the visits couldn't continue if all they did was wrestle and fight. So much for our introduction to the world of elementary-school friendships!

Friendships, whether one or many, good or bad, play a significant role in children's lives. They help shape kids' social skills and sharpen their sense of identity. In his book *Children's Friendships*, Zick Rubin writes, "The difference between a child with close friendships and a child who wants to make friends but is unable to can be the difference between a child who is happy and a child who is distressed in one large area of life."[5] How can we support their efforts to develop positive relationships with other kids? First, by realizing that the way children treat others depends on their age and stage of development, and second, by understanding that youngsters can become better friends if we are willing to help them learn about themselves and each other.

One way to encourage childhood friendships is to continue scheduling the one-on-one type of play dates you probably began during the preschool years. Setting aside this time is tough to do with our busy lifestyles, especially if there's more than one child in the family. Even though schoolchildren are around other kids all day, individual get-togethers are the only times youngsters can get to know one another without interruption. I recently realized that I had stopped inviting over playmates for my youngest son. After all, he would much rather hang around with me or his older siblings; but as they grow, his brother and sister will want more and more time to be with their own friends. Then where will the youngest be?

If you, like me, are having trouble scheduling play dates, consider these four ways to add time to your day:

- Cut back on electronic activities. Watching TV, playing video games, and playing on the computer are the least productive uses of your child's time. Why not invite a friend over on Saturday morning instead of watching cartoons?

- Drop kids' activities that don't result in friendships. Outside activities are fine, unless they take the place of close friendships. Sports and other classes afford chances to meet friends, but what good are the introductions if your child doesn't really get to know them?

- Let go of an activity that takes up your time. You need to be available to chaperone a play date. If volunteering to be a Scout leader or the treasurer of your women's group means there isn't time to invite other kids over, these activities may not be the best uses of your time.

- Be sure your child has interactive toys available to share with friends. Board games, dolls, action figures, and sports draw children together through mutual interests and allow them to interact creatively in ways that video games do not. Teach your youngster games and activities that will attract others. (Things you enjoy doing are a good place to start.)

Probably the most intensive one-on-one play date is the sleepover. Kids seem to view this kind of invitation as a rite of passage to being a "big kid." If your child is laying on a guilt trip because you haven't yet allowed her to participate, rest assured that there is a level of development before which a sleepover is *not* a good idea. Case in point: our son's first sleepover guest. Every time my son would try to engage his buddy in some type of game or activity, this child would run away and play hide-and-seek. He was very good at it! I almost had heart failure trying to find him a couple of times. My son was frustrated by this immature behavior and so was I. We mutually agreed to wait awhile before giving sleepovers another try.

What if you do all these things and your child still seems uninterested or unable to make friends? In our family there are three different levels of sociability (amazing with just three kids). We have a loner, a social butterfly, and a child who's somewhere in between. The loner is happy as long as he has one or two good friends, and even that's not always easy. The social butterfly flits from one person to another within a large circle of friends. The in-betweener interacts in a large social circle but still prefers the company of one or two special friends. Obviously our kids have differing social styles and needs for companionship, as well as for time alone. I know respecting their individuality is important, but it hasn't always been easy for me to accept these differences in their personalities.

Mothering a loner presents a particular challenge because living in community with others is important to most women. It can be hard to convince these rugged individualists simply to invite someone over. If you pressure a loner into a play date when she doesn't feel like it, the results can be disastrous—at best your child may ignore the friend; at worst you'll end up as the guest's playmate. Thank goodness studies show that kids don't need lots of close friends; one or two is enough to bolster their self-esteem and give them the chance to practice social skills. "A man of many companions may come to ruin, but there is a friend who sticks closer than a brother" (Proverbs 18:24). A child who is a loner often tends to be more introspective and perhaps more open to the introduction of Jesus as his or her ever-present friend, something all children need as they move from playing in pairs to becoming part of a group.

Belonging to a group can provide the child with a variety of resources that an individual friendship often cannot—a sense of collective participation, experience with organizational roles, and group support in the enterprise of growing up. Groups also pose for the child some of the most acute problems of social life—of inclusion and exclusion, conformity and independence.[6]

I describe the middle years' experience with group mentality as the good, the bad, and the ugly. Having your child share the fun they had playing or working together in a group is the good. They can hardly wait to tell you exactly what each person did or said! Conversely, the bad comes when your child confesses that he or she had to work or play alone because no one wanted to do something with them. Ouch! It's hard to tell who feels that pain the most, you or them. With a few exceptions, the ugly usually surfaces as the search for identity within a group intensifies. Fourth and fifth grades were the worst for the group of girls with whom my daughter "hangs." Fast friends one day, mortal enemies the next—pitting one child against another was a favorite pastime.

I felt her hurt and frustration as she related the name-calling and put-downs that seemed to be part of the daily oral language used by some of the girls. I reminded her of Jesus' words: "The greatest among you will be your servant. For whoever exalts himself will be humbled, and whoever humbles himself will be exalted" (Matthew 23:11–12). We also had the opportunity to approach these verses from the opposite perspective as I counseled her on the dangers and injustice of reciprocating with that same undesirable behavior. These skirmishes would come and go. I found it best to be supportive but not interfering. When my daughter experienced a bitter breakup with her best friend, I encouraged her not to burn bridges by saying or doing things she couldn't take back. Sure enough, after a brief hiatus, they are close friends again.

Bullying is another ugly aspect of kids' relationships that can occur individually or in a group. For me the quintessential stereotype of a bully is portrayed in the story of David and Goliath. When the Philistines and the Israelites were fighting, the Philistines wanted to decide the war through a battle between chosen champions who would meet in combat in place of the armies. The Philistines sent out their biggest, baddest bully, Goliath (who was over nine feet tall), as their champion. Twice a day for forty days, Goliath stepped forward between the armies and taunted the Israelites, who ran away in fear (1 Samuel 17:1–24). Sounds quite a bit like a playground confrontation between rival groups, doesn't it?

The basics of bullying haven't changed all that much. As with Goliath, bullies intentionally set out to hurt someone less powerful than themselves. Bullying doesn't have to be physical. It runs the gamut from hitting to name-calling to spreading rumors, and children in the middle years tend to experience it more than any other group. The effects of bullying reach beyond the antagonist and his target to bystanders, as well. Bullies come in all shapes and sizes. Their behavior differs from playful teasing in that it is intended to harm and diminish someone else's self-worth. Each of my children has been bullied, ostensibly for various reasons, such as their weight or intellect, their refusal to fight back, and their Christian beliefs.

This is one of the situations that really tests a mother's faith. In my role as mother bear, I would like nothing better than to give the bully a good tongue-lashing! Instead, as a moral and spiritual example to my child, we discuss Jesus' call to "love your enemies, do good to those who hate you, bless those who curse you, pray for those who mistreat you" (Luke 6:27–28).

In some ways this teaching has had more of a positive impact on my children than on me. My son had a girl in his class at school who took advantage of our frequent admonishment to him that "you don't hurt girls." (Remember, he has a younger sister at home.) This student was constantly hitting, pushing, or tripping him. No tactic we came up with seemed to get her to stop. One day, in frustration, I asked him why he didn't retaliate. He said earnestly, "I wouldn't hurt a lady." It took quite a bit of self-control to keep from explaining to him that this girl was no lady!

If your child is not supercommunicative, how can you tell that he or she is being bullied? Here are a few signs:

- refusing to go to school or to participate in an activity she once enjoyed

- dropping grades (it's hard to concentrate on schoolwork when you're focused on avoiding a bully)

- being excessively hungry after school (taking lunches or lunch money is a bully's favorite tactic)

- having torn or missing clothing or other possessions

- coming home with physical injuries without adequately explaining how she got them

Most kids will not admit they are being bullied without some prodding, so choose a moment (like when you're trapped together in the minivan) and ask your child if there are any bullies in class and who gets picked on. If your child tells you he is the target of a bully, let him know that it is not his fault. Emphasize that no one *ever* deserves to be hit, teased, or taunted because of their looks, actions, words, clothes, or where they live. This is also a good time to start talking about why kids act like bullies. Are they bullied at home? Do they have poor self-esteem? Have they found a surefire way to get attention? During the early elementary-school years, kids try out all sorts of new behaviors—they experiment by flexing physical and psychological muscles. Stepping in early by alerting teachers or adults in charge can nip this behavior in the bud. There are also some skills you can teach your child to help him handle those who tease and fight.

Bullying usually continues because the child being teased doesn't know how to handle it appropriately. Ineffective responses to teasing include tears, chasing after others, threatening to tell the teacher, and physically striking back. These behaviors encourage more torment because kids love to watch what happens when someone's buttons are pushed. Instead, tell your child to stay away from bullies. They can verbally respond to neutralize teasing but shouldn't get involved in one-upmanship by trying to tease back. An example response would be, "That's so old it's from the Stone Age." Kids should not physically confront a bully, including making faces; they should play close to a responsible adult if necessary. Finally, remind your child that there is strength in numbers—playing with other friends discourages a bully's advances.

What about a mom's own friendships during the middle years? Spending so much time managing your child's social calendar can leave little time for your own, but you can't relegate your relationships to the backseat of the minivan. One of my girlfriends recently sent me an e-mail article about a UCLA study on the health benefits of friendships among women. "Scientists now suspect that hanging out with our friends can counteract the kind of stomach-quivering stress most of us experience on a daily basis. Women respond to stress with a cascade of brain chemicals that cause us to make and maintain friendships with other women."[7] Studies show that being with friends causes the release of more chemicals that counter stress and produce a calming effect. Friends are good for our health and our sanity.

I've discovered new friends lately whom I affectionately refer to as my extracurricular cronies, or ECCs (also a reminder of the friendship verse at the beginning of the chapter: Ecclesiastes 4:10). These are the moms you sit next to on bleachers at T-ball games, whisper to while observing your budding ballerina at the studio, or roll down the window of the car to chat with while waiting in the piano teacher's driveway. These friends share our daily struggles. They are an important part of our information and support network. Talking with them makes us feel connected and gives us a much-needed break from the isolation of our daily drives.

In her book *In the Company of Women*, Dr. Brenda Hunter discusses why friendships are essential. "Our family relationships require work. We sometimes struggle to be the responsive mother, the dutiful daughter, and the intimate wife. Most of us have a hard time keeping all the relational balls we juggle in the air. But when it comes to our friends, we can generally relax. Friends are the support players who usually require fewer emotional supplies than family members and who help us with our problems."[8] In spite of all the rushing around moms do during this stage of life, we need friends. Whether it's reestablishing old relationships or enjoying regular contact with new extracurricular cronies, time with friends is time well spent.

The writer of Hebrews recognized the importance of the

spiritual and emotional support provided by friends when he wrote, "Let us consider how we may spur one another on toward love and good deeds. Let us not give up meeting together. . .but let us encourage one another" (Hebrews 10:24–25). Our children crave this kind of love and affirmation just as we do.

Mom's Moments

My daughter gets a kick out of the fact that I occasionally go out to dinner or to see a show with my friends. Spending time with "the girls" demonstrates the importance you place on friendship and models every mom's need for time to herself.

Moms are not immune to the good, the bad, and the ugly of relationships. When friendship troubles occur, remember that you have a constant friend who will always be there to help, so you can know and rely on the love of God (1 John 4:16).

Are you a loner, a social butterfly, or somewhere in between? Consider how your socialization comfort level differs from your child and what signals that may be sending to him or her.

Things That Go Bump in the Night

I sought the LORD, and he answered me;
he delivered me from all my fears.

PSALM 34:4

One of my favorite Disney movies in recent memory is *Monsters, Inc.*, which tells the story of a little girl and the scary, yet basically good-hearted, monster in her closet. I liked the way it encouraged kids of all ages not to be afraid of things that go bump in the night, especially since all three of my children refuse to sleep without a light on. My daughter, Shelby, actually has a pretty good excuse. There's a large closet off of her room—the kind that you're afraid to open because all the junk will fall out and crush you! Despite the possibility of all kinds of things lurking in that closet, my daughter was not afraid to sleep without a light. Then one evening, our cat snuck into the closet while I was shoving in some outgrown clothes. Just as Shelby was dropping off to sleep, the cat jumped on an unsteady pile of stuff, which fell over with a large *crash*, causing the cat to howl and hiss. Needless to say, it was an event that scarred my daughter for life. Since that fateful night, the closet door must be barricaded and the night-light on before she will even consider going to bed.

I have a confession to make: Since childhood, I have been afraid of the dark, too. My fear began as a youngster's typical aversion to lying down in a room at night by myself and not being able to see what was going on around me (which was, of course, nothing). Solution: night-light. As I grew older, this fear was fed by a fascination with the science-fiction shows and stories so prevalent in the 1970s. There was always some alien or monster waiting to emerge from under my bed to do. . .what? I didn't want to find out, and the light in the hall was the only thing that kept these imaginary intruders at bay.

As I became a young woman living on my own, there were other fears about the dark, like people outside the window or in the alley. Now, nothing bad has *ever* happened to me at night (unless you count the three times I woke up in labor), but somehow, all those years of positive experience didn't neutralize my fear. Not until I was quite a bit older did I realize that I wasn't afraid of the dark but of the unknown and unseen.

My husband is just the opposite. He *has* to sleep with the room as dark as possible. Even though I was a bit uncomfortable in pitch blackness, I felt safe sleeping with him because someone strong, whom I could trust, was next to me. Only my deepening relationship with the Lord has allowed me to accept that there are good things that are unseen. "We fix our eyes not on what is seen, but on what is unseen. For what is seen is temporary, but what is unseen is eternal" (2 Corinthians 4:18). Regardless of my fear, there is always someone powerful and trustworthy next to me even if I can't see Him.

"I will lie down and sleep in peace, for you alone, O Lord, make me dwell in safety" (Psalm 4:8). This verse may soothe us, but it's almost impossible for school-age children to make that leap of faith from what they've seen to the unseen. As Stanley Greenspan writes in *The Secure Child*:

> *School-age children will often have more intense fears and worries than their preschool counterparts do. This is because they can now more fully appreciate a danger seen on TV or covered in the newspaper or overheard from parents. The danger isn't just a fleeting image, as with a preschooler; it's one that they can hold onto and examine. However, children at this age don't yet have the tools to assess this danger in terms of the likelihood of it happening to them. They know too much but do not yet have the coping capacities to deal with what they know.*[9]

Our children's fears, stresses, and worries manifest themselves in unusual ways, particularly when it comes to nighttime. For a while, one of our kids experienced night terrors, which was terrifying for us all. An hour after going to bed, he would sit bolt upright, eyes wide open, and start screaming. We quickly learned not to try to wake him (since that was ineffective) but just to hold or sit next to him until the episode was over. After about ten minutes, he would calm down and not remember a thing the next day. Another child was a sleepwalker who would come downstairs at least once a week and say something puzzling like, "I need to get the *thing*." One evening we heard a noise and climbed the stairs to find her trying to climb the wall in the hallway! She also remembered nothing the next day. Even though we were used to reacting quickly to a child in distress, our middle-years children kept us jumping up off the couch long after we thought we'd be finished with bedtime battles.

The difference between these night disturbances and other fears was that I never knew their cause. I could understand a fear of bugs, of putting your head underwater, or of unfamiliar people, but being unable to identify a fear made it difficult to know what to do. Thankfully, kids usually outgrow both night terrors and sleepwalking. If your child has frequent nightmares or exhibits other excessive fears, try these suggestions to help her feel more secure:

Reassure your child. If your child wakes up afraid, stay with her until she is calm. Give extra hugs and opportunities for cuddle time in the evening to help her feel more secure.

Encourage your child to talk during the day about things that bother him. Acknowledge your youngster's feelings and discuss them openly. Help him work through a fear by putting it in perspective with factual information. For example, if your child says he had a bad dream about someone kidnapping him, let him know it's good to be cautious, but few children are actually taken away by strangers each year. Don't make light of your child's fear or tease him about it.

Don't transfer your own fears. Children are very astute at picking up on our insecurities and fears. Try not to convey your own anxieties when discussing your child's fears with him.

Protect your child against frightening images in the media. Violent or scary movies and gruesome images in the evening news can cause bedtime fears and contribute to a fearful view of the world. These fears can persist for months or years. I saw Alfred Hitchcock's *Psycho* as an adult and still get jittery when taking a shower in the house by myself!

Give kids opportunities to help others. Let them reassure a younger sibling or cousin about one of their fears. Have them run errands for a grandparent or help them do light housework or yard work.

What about our own fears? As my children have become increasingly independent from me, I find myself worrying more about the injuries others might inflict on them. Even in our own small town, where crime usually consists of vandalism or automobile accidents, there have been several attempts to abduct children from their yards or off the sidewalk (apparently perpetrated by out-of-towners). If you can't trust your kids will be safe in small-town America, can you relax anywhere?

We need to teach our kids to heed scripture's age-old advice: "My son, preserve sound judgment and discernment, do not let them out of your sight; they will be life for you. . . . Then you will go on your way in safety" (Proverbs 3:21–23). Today it's not enough for children to be school smart; their safety depends on them being street smart, as well. Kids in elementary school can understand that some adults may wish to harm them, but they usually think they can identify a "bad" person by the way that person looks. Movies and television often portray dangerous individuals as strangers who are dirty, ugly, or deformed. They may speak strangely or act suspiciously. In real life, children are much more likely to be abducted or abused by someone who knows your family.

Help your children develop sound judgment about other adults by teaching them to be S.A.F.E.:

Strangers asking for help should be avoided. There are many lures predators use to attract children. Abductors want to trick their victims into going with them willingly. Let your child know that she should never go with a stranger to look for a lost kitten or puppy or approach someone in a car who is asking for directions. Adults needing directions should ask other adults. If an adult approaches them, kids should say no to their request and hurry to tell you or another safe adult.

Always stay with a buddy. There's safety in numbers. If your child is old enough to go places close by on his own, make sure he has friends with him.

Follow your own feelings. I once read that children who have been taught to think for themselves are the safest children of all. All kids have some level of instinct or intuition that helps keep them safe. Encourage them to trust their own feelings about people and the things they are asked to do.

Every experience is okay to talk about. Keeping the lines of communication open helps kids avoid problems that can result from being too friendly or cooperative with adults who may harm them. The fear of punishment may make your child reluctant to tell you about a problem she encountered at a house you've forbidden her to visit. Let her know she can *always* talk to you.

As the saying goes, "Forewarned is forearmed," but don't overdo the scary stories and frighten your child. Instead play "what if" to teach her how to handle situations she may encounter. Point out safe places your child can go and people who will help if she is lost or scared. As Helen Keller once declared, "Life is either a daring adventure or nothing. Security does not exist in nature, nor do the children of men as a whole experience it. Avoiding danger is no safer in the long run than exposure." Provide controlled experiences to foster your youngster's sense of independence and feelings of self-confidence. For example, walk with her down the street to a friend's house several times, then stand in the driveway and watch her walk, then take a deep breath and watch from the window as she walks on her own.

Nurturing your child's self-esteem is just as important in this season as in the early years, because research shows that kids experience a significant drop in self-esteem when they enter first grade. In his book *Self-Esteem Revolutions in Children*, Dr. Thomas Phelan gives three main reasons for this decline:

1. *Self-esteem starts to be related to real performance in the real world.* It is now also based upon competence.
2. How well a child is doing is measured not just against how well he or she was doing before, *but also against how well other kids in their class or age group are doing.*
3. The unconditional love of parents finds a new mate: *the conditional love and acceptance of other people,* such as peers and teachers.[10]

Moms can shore up kids' self-esteem by commenting on the things they *can* do instead of those they can't. Even when it's hard to appreciate some aspects of your child's temperament, don't make comments that convey the message you disapprove of him or her. (These often are the same traits we dislike in ourselves.) The middle years give kids many opportunities to boost their own self-confidence by accomplishing new tasks, but there's also a fear factor to becoming more independent.

Some first-time fears, like the first day of each new grade in school, can be lessened by planning ahead together—visiting your student's new classroom, meeting the teacher, and getting all her school supplies together before the beginning of the term. Other fears, if not addressed, lead to bad habits that become harder to break over time. I've noticed an interesting by-product of the fear of failure in my own children. This fear results in two completely opposite kinds of behavior: perfectionism and procrastination.

"Remember that fear always lurks behind perfectionism.

Confronting your fears and allowing yourself the right to be human can, paradoxically, make you a far happier and more productive person," says Dr. David Burns. Does anyone else have a student who obsesses over making less than straight As in school? Parents can instill a desire for perfection in their children, but individual temperament may also lead kids to develop perfectionist standards for themselves. I'm proud of my child's accomplishments, but sometimes I wonder: *Have we created a monster?* A fixation on doing everything perfectly makes us fearful because there are only two possibilities, perfection or failure. Not allowing yourself to be human and to make mistakes leads to being overly critical—not the happiest or healthiest of conditions.

On the flip side, we also have a child who has honed procrastination to a fine art. I'm not sure which reason applies more to his affinity for the word *later*. Is it the fear that his work won't be good enough or simply the enjoyment of pushing my buttons by putting off something I've asked him to do? Not that I have a tendency to procrastinate. (Right now I'm looking at a basket of clean laundry that's needed to be put away for several days and the outdated decorations still waiting to be boxed up from our most recent holiday!) Don Marquis observed that "procrastination is the art of keeping up with yesterday." If we were behind by only one day, most of us would be very happy indeed.

For me, fighting the tendency toward either perfectionism or procrastination comes down to one verse from scripture, "God did not give us a spirit of timidity, but a spirit of power, of love and of self-discipline" (2 Timothy 1:7). When fear intimidates or paralyzes us, it keeps us from being or doing our best as God intended. The story of Daniel and the lions' den gives us a powerful example of how faith overcomes fear. Daniel defied King Darius's decree that his subjects could pray only to him (upon pain of death). Even though Darius had great affection for Daniel, the king ordered that he be thrown into the lions' den for his disobedience.

Now, I've been to the zoo many times. I'd be scared to death to do anything that would put me in an enclosed area with those magnificent animals, well fed or not! Regardless of the fear Daniel might have felt about the consequences of his actions, he remained faithful, and God rewarded that faith by saving Daniel's life. By delivering Daniel, God demonstrated His power to the king and all the people of the land. Faith kept Daniel from being intimidated and allowed him to accomplish God's plan. The lesson from Daniel's story is that the Lord doesn't want us to be afraid of anything, even death. Our faith gives us the power and self-discipline to overcome fear and live life to the fullest as God intends.

At every stage in our kids' lives there are things that make us fearful—health concerns when they're little, safety concerns as they grow. When worry overwhelms you, it may feel like an act of will to get through the day. Consider this: Whose will am I relying on, mine or God's? The apostle Paul wrote, "I can do everything through him who gives me strength" (Philippians 4:13). By teaching our children to turn their fears over to the Lord, we introduce them to the biggest, strongest source of power available to them. In time they'll learn what we already know: No matter where we go, who we're with, or what challenges we face, day or night the Lord always leaves the light on for us.

Mom's Moments

Is there a fear you have yet to conquer for yourself or for your child? Examine the root of that fear. You may have to look into your past for its source and then ask God for His strength and healing to overcome it.

Before bed, say this prayer with your child, then turn on the night-light:

The Lord is my light and my salvation—whom shall I fear? The Lord is the stronghold of my life—of whom shall I be afraid? (Psalm 27:1).

Don't let a fear of failure keep you from accomplishing all that God has in store for your life. Tap into the same self-discipline you draw from to meet your mothering responsibilities, and apply it to your personal goals.

Sportsmanlike Conduct

*"What good is it for a man to gain the whole world,
and yet lose or forfeit his very self?"*

LUKE 9:25

I am not a sports person, or at least I wasn't as a child. Our family overwhelmingly consisted of women. My father was an only child. I have just one sister. My mother had one sister, and my aunt has two daughters. Males were definitely in the minority at all family functions. Growing up before the passage of laws designed to promote equality in the availability of girls' sports in public schools, I directed my time and energy toward the more acceptable pursuits of music and dance. Thank goodness times have changed and women have made progress toward leveling the playing field. (My father balanced our artsy activities by taking us camping, canoeing, and sailing.) I've provided this brief family history so you'll believe me when I say that I had never been indoctrinated into the sports culture—until my children started playing T-ball.

I'd been to my share of sporting events as a spectator, but I really had *no* idea what to expect from elementary-school sports. I assumed that my kindergartener with the hat and glove too large for the respective parts of his body would hit, catch, and throw. Those are the basics of baseball, right? Instead, we had what my husband affectionately refers to as a "daisy picker." Game after game, my son was more interested in the dandelions than what was happening near home plate. The ball occasionally would roll or bounce past him in the outfield as he obliviously daydreamed or conversed with his nearest neighbor.

He was adorable, but I was too uptight to notice. Between me encouraging him to pay attention during the game and the postgame analysis, I'm sure my son caught on to my anxiety about his performance. I acted like the stereotypical sports mom. The only good thing I can say about my attitude is that it improved with practice. By the time our third child was in T-ball, we both got a lot of what sports should give kids in the middle years: a good time.

We signed our kids up for youth sports programs for most of the right reasons:

- to satisfy his or her interest in the sport

- to provide an opportunity to interact with other youngsters

- to learn how to be part of a team

- to encourage exercise

- to learn how to win and lose

Sometimes it seemed we forgot the most important reason for a child to be involved in any extracurricular activity—*to have fun*. I started with the best intentions, but all that time spent driving to a practice, game, or event, followed by hours sitting on the bleachers or in a folding chair watching my child not give it his all (and to pay for the privilege), started to grate on me.

In *Raising a Team Player*, Harry Sheehy says parents approach youth sports the right way when they understand that "developing a strong value system is more important than winning. Being a team player is more important than being a good scorer, and the most important reason that kids play sports is because it's fun. When it stops being fun, they'll stop wanting to play and they'll stop learning."[11] Unfortunately, if you've attended a game or match lately, you've probably noticed that this often is not what youth sports is about. Those of us who have been only armchair quarterbacks or pitchers or goalies have allowed the expectations of and attitudes toward professional sports to spill over into our children's games.

Kids can learn a lot from being involved in youth sports, as long as the program (and the overinvested parent) takes into consideration the specific attributes of their stage of development. For example, most six- and some seven-year-olds cannot lose at a competition without blowing up. Yet many sports programs keep score in contests from preschool age on. Obviously, this is setting up the participants for tears and tantrums, unsportsmanlike behavior, and general hard feelings. It's only from age eight and beyond that children can be expected to handle the thrill of victory and the agony of defeat. Good sportsmanship begins at home when you emphasize fun over winning and losing, whether you're playing a board game or some type of sports activity. It may sound trite, but we've encouraged our kids from an early age to honor their opponents with a "Good game" and a handshake after a contest. There's nothing wrong with the desire to win; it's only when we place winning above all else that it's a problem.

In 1 Corinthians 9:24–25, Paul writes, "Do you not know that in a race all the runners run, but only one gets the prize? Run in such a way as to get the prize. Everyone who competes in the games goes into strict training. They do it to get a crown that will not last; but we do it to get a crown that will last forever." When children participate in extracurricular activities, we can help train up their character so that they participate in life God's way and are eligible for the prize waiting for them at the end. Use these guidelines to promote "good sports" character in your family:

Teach good sportsmanship. Remind kids often to show respect for their own teammates as well as the other team. A good sport also congratulates the winners and tries to help those who lose feel better. You can do your part by not letting the first words out of your mouth be "Did you win?" Instead, ask questions like "Did you have fun?" or "What do you think we should work on together this week?"

Talk about specific incidents. Teachable moments abound when your child is involved in extracurricular activities. When negative behavior occurs on the part of your child or someone else, discuss the circumstances and talk about how things could have been handled differently. If your child is the one engaged in taunting or other obnoxious behavior, take him aside quietly and remind him how a good sport should act. Don't compound the situation by embarrassing him in front of the other kids. Role-play other possible scenarios with your youngster. What should she do when a person on the opposing team calls her a bad name, a parent yells at his child during the game, or she feels a referee's call was unfair?

Encourage, encourage, encourage. The word *encourage* literally means "to give courage, confidence, or hope" to someone. That doesn't mean you shouldn't point out areas that can be improved, but those comments should be balanced with lots of positive reinforcement. Emphasize effort and improvement, not winning. Require consistency in good behavior at home and during practices as well as during a game or contest. Under pressure, people tend to revert to learned behaviors. By insisting on good sportsmanship in all circumstances, you are more likely to observe it in your child at game time.

Be a good role model. For kids to be good sports, we have to lead the way by modeling positive behaviors and actions. There were teams we always were unhappy about playing because of their history of poor sportsmanship. This kind of attitude is transferred from the top down, from parents and coaches to kids. Be a good fan by making sure you root for your child or team and not against the opponents. On more than one occasion, we have had to assure our competitive kids that we are not traitors if we clap for good plays made by the other team. If we adults adopt an attitude of "do as I say, not as I do" with respect to sportsmanship, everything else we try to teach our kids about the subject will be in vain.

There's the rub, because children's activities often seem to bring out childish behavior in adults. How often have you heard someone say, "I really enjoy the kids—it's the other parents who drive me crazy!" Why do we hear all these stories about spectators (almost always adults) yelling at kids, coaches, and referees? We get caught up in the excitement of competition. We're too invested and living vicariously through our kids. Most importantly, we forget that *it's just a game*, and not even our game at that, but our child's.

I've experienced youth sports from three different sides—as the mom of a non-sports-inclined kid, the mom of an athletically gifted child, and the wife of a coach. Each circumstance has presented its own unique struggles, but I must admit the position I found most challenging was as the coach's wife. My husband has coached each of our children in the kindergarten through second-grade level of T-ball. At one of our very first games, some confusion brewed as to whether a child on the other team had legally scored a run or not. My husband told the opposing coach to count the child's run to home plate because he felt it was more important to fuel a kid's enthusiasm for the game than to keep score. One parent from our team did not agree with this generosity and spent the rest of the game yelling at my husband from the sidelines. As I was seeing red, all I could think was, *Get real! These kids can't count the score. Why are you worrying about it?* Given the general chaos inherent in children's activities, someone has to act like an adult; it might as well be you.

To truly enjoy youth sports, perhaps parents should see them more from their kids' perspectives—including daisy pickers. By focusing on fun, not runs or goals or points, we help children gain the character of a winner. During the last Olympic Games, my daughter and I were watching an awards ceremony. She told me how sorry she felt for one of the participants who received "only the silver medal." I started thinking, *What's wrong with being the second fastest person in the world?* Win or lose, people who are successful find positives in their situation. This is the type of wisdom we should impart to our budding baseball or soccer players, our dancers and gymnasts. "Then [they] will understand what is right and just and fair—every good path" (Proverbs 2:9).

Despite the petty aggravations, most parents agree that extracurricular activities provide positives to kids' lives. The bigger question often becomes, how many? Like a candy store is to a child, every opportunity to expand our young-sters' horizons looks tempting. Dance, Little League, piano, karate, chess, gymnastics. . .since you don't really know where your child's aptitudes and interests lie, it's best to let her try as many different things as possible, right? That depends on the pace of life in your house and the level of stress it creates. Most of us overcrowd our lives such that we are always in a hurry, and so are our children. Scripture tells us, "Woe. . .to those who say, 'Let God hurry, let him hasten his work so we may see it' " (Isaiah 5:18–19).

As Dr. Bettie Youngs writes in her book *Stress and Your Child*, "Rushing children and rushing childhood have conse-quences. Children's games are rapidly disappearing. Play for play's sake is gone. Whatever happened to the *fun* of just being a child?"[12] There are many reasons why moms enroll their kids in every available activity:

- to give them opportunities that weren't available to us

- to let them try out something they have an interest in

- to give a child a jump start on becoming a champion

- to make sure they are well prepared for the future

In and of itself, each of these rationales is valid, but we forget to live in the real world where time is usually in scarce supply. What moms really need is for someone to tell us to get a grip on ourselves and remember that providing opportunities at the expense of quality of life is not really a gift for our children. Who wants to be trapped in the minivan—at least any more than necessary?

As parents, it's up to us to help our kids maintain balance in the middle years, to protect them from doing too much too soon. Look over Dr. Youngs's checklist of five things to consider in determining if you are pushing your child too hard:

- How many hours a day does your child spend in downtime?

- How many hours a week are devoted to extracurricular lessons of any sort, including sports?

- Does your child eat most of his evening meals at home or elsewhere?

- Does your child have trouble remembering all the activities he is in or what activity is scheduled for what day?

- What hobbies does your child have at home? What projects has he started at home?[13]

How much is too much differs from family to family and child to child; some require more downtime than others. When we first began limiting our children's commitments, our benchmark was two activities per child. (If you do the math, with our three kids that comes out to six activities total.) This plan quickly turned out to be more of a guideline than a hard-and-fast rule. Many activities available to kids in the middle years run for only a set period of time. For example, where we live, soccer season is from August to October, and basketball runs from January to March. Both sports involve one afternoon practice and one Saturday game a week. Our youngest son takes piano lessons and is a member of a Cub Scout troop. If we stuck with the "only two" activities rule, he would not be able to be involved in sports. So we bend the rule a bit and allow three activities at a time as long as one of the activities requires a commitment of only a couple of months. Sounds like one of those math word problems, doesn't it? "What's the maximum number of extracurricular things Spencer, Shelby, and Ross can participate in before they drive Mom and her van over the edge?" Ours is not a perfect system! How do other families handle this dilemma? One of my friends encourages her children to choose one sport, one church-related activity, and one other extracurricular activity to provide balance to their pursuits.

It only makes sense that the more kids there are in a family, the more restrictions you may have to impose. Another thing to consider is whether or not you expect siblings to attend at least some of each other's games and performances, as we do. Time spent supporting one another must also be factored into already crowded schedules. It would be nice if we could blame all this hurrying around solely on our youngsters, but most of us contribute mightily to the chaos with our own extracurriculars. Kids take their cues from us. As

Beth Wilson Saavedra writes in *Creating Balance in Your Child's Life*, "When we slow down, our children slow down, and we have the wonderful opportunity to connect with those we love. Instead of time being a scarce commodity to be doled out and used up, we can create time to move at the speed of life—not the speed of light."[14]

How many activities are you involved in? One way to tell if you're overextended is to look at the state of your spiritual life. When my family is too busy, I usually find myself cutting out things of my own that add to the schedule. I'm embarrassed to admit that personal quiet time spent in reflection, reading scripture, and prayer is one of the first things to be put on the back burner—and just when I need it the most! The biblical story of Mary and Martha is my favorite because it's about one woman who hurried to finish her to-do list and another who knew when to stop and listen to God. I feel particularly close to Martha because we're so much alike. See if you recognize yourself in one of these women.

> *As Jesus and his disciples were on their way, he came to a village where a woman named Martha opened her home to him. She had a sister called Mary, who sat at the Lord's feet listening to what he said. But Martha was distracted by all the preparations that had to be made. She came to him and asked, "Lord, don't you care that my sister has left me to do the work by myself? Tell her to help me!"*
>
> *"Martha, Martha," the Lord answered, "you are worried and upset about many things, but only one thing is needed. Mary has chosen what is better, and it will not be taken away from her" (Luke 10:38–42).*

Many of us scaled back on our time with the Lord when we were constantly on call during our children's early years. This is the season to renew and revitalize that relationship! If you cut out just one volunteer activity or membership in one women's group, consider what you could have time for—studying the Bible, joining a prayer chain, setting aside your own time daily to sit at the Lord's feet. Like Martha, I find myself becoming addicted to being busy, then I wonder why I have headaches or stomachaches or trouble sleeping, why I feel trapped and angry (all signs of stress).

Keeping my own schedule in check leaves me time to meet intimately with God, to "hurry to my place of shelter, far from the tempest and storm" (Psalm 55:8). It also allows me to lighten up and have fun with my children. The middle years are precious because no class or activity can take the place of time your kids spend with you. What good does it do us to give our kids every opportunity if they withdraw from us because we're not available to them? What good is it for us to be involved in all kinds of worthy causes if we lose or forfeit ourselves? In life, as in kids' sports, it's not whether we win or lose, but how we play the game that counts.

Mom's Moments

Studies show that symptoms of stress disappear when parents reduce the number of kids' commitments and allow them to participate in deciding which classes or activities to get involved in. It's never too late to pare down—you'll free up family time and money!

I saw a bumper sticker recently that read, "What part of rest in Him don't I understand?" The Lord doesn't want us to miss enjoying life in the rush of doing. If rest seems out of reach, build it into your schedule just like any other activity.

"Watch out that you do not lose what you have worked for, but that you may be rewarded fully. Anyone who runs ahead and does not continue in the teaching of Christ does not have God; whoever continues in the teaching has both the Father and the Son" (2 John 8–9). Are you rushing through life? Take time to study Christ's teachings so you can keep reaching for the prize.

True
Lies

Trust in the Lord with all your heart
and lean not on your own understanding.

PROVERBS 3:5

Did you feed the cats? Yup. Have you made your bed? Uh-huh. Is your homework finished? Yes, Mom. These responses make my kids sound too good to be true, which is why I shouldn't be surprised that they are not always honest. Those entertaining "whoppers" from the preschool years have given way to more mundane, harder-to-spot untruths. I am fortunate that my children are three of the *worst* liars I've ever seen. It's something about their eyes or the way they hold their mouths—I can almost always tell when they are trying to put one over on me. I usually find out about the times I've missed a white lie because it's impossible to get away with things when you live in a small town. Despite the fact that they are always found out, along with my constant reminders that "telling the truth gets you into less trouble than telling a lie," my kids continue testing my powers of intuition (and the power of local gossip) by telling small untruths.

As a mother, I wonder, *Where did I go wrong?*

Uncovering the reasons for lying is the first step in deciding how to respond in order to discourage your child from lying again. Studies show that the main reason kids lie is to avoid punishment, but there are plenty of other reasons, such as protecting friends or siblings from trouble, getting something they couldn't get otherwise, or avoiding embarrassment. My children have been evasive about a stain on the carpet (they're not allowed to drink outside of the kitchen) or whether they snuck some candy before supper, plus a host of other small falsehoods.

Training my kids that true confession would yield only a verbal reminder of the house rules and the opportunity to fix what was broken or clean up what was spilled—versus facing the wrath of Mommy for telling a lie—has been an uphill battle. Society as a whole has become much more lax in its tolerance of lying, and that has translated even into small lies I've made to make my life more convenient. It's tempting to tell the telemarketer I'm too busy to be disturbed rather than go through my spiel about how our family has a policy of not buying things by phone. If someone with whom I have little in common asks me to go to lunch, my conflict over hurting their feelings is easily resolved if I think up some plausible excuse for why I can't go. Our children observe these little social lies, which can become the basis for a habit of telling small untruths that leads to bigger lies.

A friend told this real-life example of how her children learned about honesty through her actions:

> *One day we went through the McDonald's drive-thru and the girl at the window handed me two dollars too much in change. When I gave it back to her, my girls asked, "Why'd you give it back, Mom?" I told them that the employee had just made an error, and I owed her that two dollars' change—it wasn't right for me to keep it. We just went on our way, but I knew that made an impression on them.*

Scripture clearly states that lying is not acceptable. "The Lord detests lying lips, but he delights in men who are truthful" (Proverbs 12:22). Isaiah wrote poetically about the consequences of dishonesty, "Justice is driven back, and righteousness stands at a distance; truth has stumbled in the streets, honesty cannot enter" (Isaiah 59:14). The first time I caught each of my kids in a lie, I felt shocked, then angry, then betrayed. How could they? It was tempting to come down on them hard, to nip this undesirable behavior in the bud. Is that the right course to take?

In *Why Kids Lie*, Dr. Paul Ekman encourages parents not to respond in anger; instead, try to understand the motive for the lying:

> *Very often that understanding will allow you to talk to your child in a way that will allow the child to be truthful, which will eliminate the child's motive for*

lying. It may require no more than acknowledging some
misdeed your child has done. Show forgiveness.
Remember what it was like when you were a child.
This doesn't mean giving up your rules or standards,
but it does mean understanding rather than always
punishing any infraction. And, as your child grows
older, it means being willing to discuss or negotiate the
rules you live by as a family.[15]

This doesn't mean lying shouldn't have its consequences. Our policy is that a youngster may or may not be punished for the misdeed he or she lied about (depending on the type and severity), but there will be a consequence for the lie. From time to time, I have not called a child on a blatant mistruth in order to give guilt time to do its work. Often my child will contritely approach me later to tell me what really happened. In those cases, the consequence is my explanation of how lies destroy trust and without my trust, "you probably will not be able to do some things you'd like to do." As distasteful as we find lying, it isn't the end of the world as long as it isn't chronic. However, if we try to corner our children and overreact in frustration when they don't come clean, we actually teach them how to become better liars!

If you want to bring a child's problem with honesty before the Lord, first talk with him about how God can help us change our hearts. Then pray together, "Since you are my rock and my fortress, for the sake of your name lead and guide me. . .for you are my refuge. Into your hands I commit my spirit; redeem me, O Lord, the God of truth" (Psalm 31:3–5).

"Catch" your children telling the truth from time to time

and give them praise. If you think they may be embarking on a tall tale, before the lie comes out, stop them with a gentle reminder of "Remember, it's important to tell the truth."

Honesty is just one of the virtues moms want to nurture in their youngsters. Here are some others we value in our family:

- Courage
- Humor
- Self-reliance
- Dependability
- Respect
- Cooperation
- Unselfishness
- Discipline

Let's take a look at each of these virtues in turn.

Courage. The ability to overcome our fear is something we all possess to one extent or another. Doing the right thing in the face of criticism or taunting is another way we display courage. Our children need to see us step in and speak up against those things we oppose and take a stand for the principles in which we believe. Courage could also be defined as "taking a risk when the objective is worthwhile." Peter once took a great risk to reach Jesus across a body of water:

During the fourth watch of the night Jesus went out to them, walking on the lake. When the disciples saw him

walking on the lake, they were terrified. "It's a ghost,"
they said, and cried out in fear. But Jesus immediately
said to them: "Take courage! It is I. Don't be afraid."
"Lord, if it's you," Peter replied, "tell me to come to you
on the water." "Come," he said. Then Peter got down
out of the boat, walked on the water and came toward
Jesus (Matthew 14:25–29).

Although Peter initially acted in faith, his courage wavered, and he began to sink. Living without courage makes us feel weak and unequal to the tasks before us. Giving your child generous praise when she completes a difficult task increases her confidence, even if it takes years to become noticeable. My daughter had an accident on her first day of second grade when she broke off part of her front tooth. This traumatic and painful experience was not eased by the even more traumatic (but painless) trip to the dentist. The next regularly scheduled trip to the dentist resulted in quite a battle complete with much begging and tears. However, the positive reinforcement she received during and after the appointment made the next dental visit slightly less stressful. After several years, we've finally gotten to the point where she just says, "I hate going to the dentist," on the way to the appointment.

Kids need courage to combat the negative influences bombarding them today. We illustrate that kind of courage by expressing our beliefs, even if they aren't popular, and by being transparent enough to talk about situations when we felt courageous. When the time came for my oldest son to give his first oral report in elementary school, parents were invited. I sat in the back of the room so as not to make him more nervous.

Afterward I told him what a good job he did and shared how I was absolutely petrified at my first public speaking engagement. His response: "Oh, I didn't really feel nervous at all!"

My daughter was more understanding when I explained how it takes a lot of courage for me to eliminate a spider from the house each time she screams over one (arachnophobia is a fear we share). Another way to boost your courage as well as your child's is to read books together about people who have acted courageously, like Martin Luther King or Corrie ten Boom. It even takes courage to admit when we are wrong— certainly an important quality to impart. Here are some other things to keep in mind:

Humor. A good sense of humor is one of the most attractive traits. People who find comedy in everyday life seem to be more resilient in the face of adversity. Studies even show that laughter strengthens your immune system and helps with healing. Author and humorist Mark Twain wrote, "Always do right. This will gratify some people, and astonish the rest." Have you ever astonished your kids by making a joke out of a mistake? One of my favorite stories from my childhood comes from our family kitchen. My mother, who always has been a fantastic cook, once sprinkled cayenne pepper instead of paprika over the baked chicken. You can imagine the scene her two young daughters made after eating some: choking, sputtering, and begging for more water. This story came in handy during one of my own, more frequent cooking disasters. I could laugh as my children were gulping water, because no matter how much pepper I put in a dish, it will never be as hot as my mother's chicken paprika!

Continue being playful with your child. Middle-years kids love slapstick humor and practical jokes. (You will have to judge and set guidelines for how far these antics should go.) Many youngsters use humor to diffuse tension or anxiety. Sometimes their stories and jokes border on the inappropriate; potty humor is big at this stage. Try not to overreact, but do set limits, especially if their comments are disrespectful of others.

Self-reliance. As moms, we work with our children toward the goal of self-reliance from birth until they leave the nest. In the middle years, it's helpful to think of yourself more as a consultant than a manager of your child's life, someone who is available to help but not make every choice for him. Give your child plenty of opportunities to do things for himself: make his own lunch, choose his clothes, call a friend to invite him over, or find his own entertainment (not TV, computer, or video-game related).

Encourage your child *not* to always follow the crowd by giving her opportunities to make her own decisions. Be sure to praise each positive decision. A solid foundation in God's Word provides the basis for good judgment, which in turn gives kids confidence to think and act independently. "All Scripture is God-breathed and is useful for teaching, rebuking, correcting and training in righteousness, so that the man of God may be thoroughly equipped for every good work" (2 Timothy 3:16–17). The book of Proverbs provides short, to-the-point wisdom about what is right, just, and fair. Read passages from this book at dinner and discuss them with your children to impart true spiritual values.

Be the embodiment of self-reliance for your children. Do you leave even simple household projects to your husband's expertise? Does your youngster see you try new things or persevere when the going gets tough? Successful or not, sometimes the lesson of self-reliance is best taught when kids observe us trying.

Dependability. Demonstrating love and constancy to our children—that's part of a mom's daily job description. Think of the numerous, largely unsung instances just today when you've shown yourself to be dependable. Your family may not even be aware of the things you do for them, but they certainly notice if you fail to appear. Many of us, myself included, have forgotten to pick up a child from an activity; more of us have been late. Don't allow infrequent lapses to derail your own feelings of dependability.

Be sure to remind kids of all the times you have been there and all the things you do for them. Better yet, highlight visible examples of your dependability as they occur. For example, tell your child, "No matter what I have to do that afternoon, I'll be at your game because it's important to me to support you." When kids exhibit dependable behaviors, let them know you appreciate their effort. Remind them that, as human beings, we are all prone to making mistakes. However, God's character and promises are completely dependable. "My salvation and my honor depend on God; he is my mighty rock, my refuge" (Psalm 62:7). The Lord is strong even in our weakness.

> *Respect.* Aretha Franklin sang, "R-E-S-P-E-C-T. Find out what it means to me." Have you taken the time to explain what *respect* means to your children? My favorite definitions are "to regard with esteem or honor" and "to treat with consideration." Children do not learn respect unless it is first given to them. Often we treat our family with less consideration than we treat strangers, but respect comes naturally if we follow the Golden Rule: Do unto others as you would have them do unto you. By listening politely to our children's opinions, asking permission to use one of their belongings, and honoring their privacy, we help them develop the equally important quality of self-respect. By building their self-respect, we hope our children will feel proud of their own words and actions.

As we treat our kids respectfully, they should behave in kind. We tell our children that there are many ways to act with disrespect besides just saying no to a parent's reasonable request. In addition to words, tone of voice, posture, and eye contact all convey how they really feel. In their book *Teaching Your Children Values*, Linda and Richard Eyre encourage parents to correct behavior in a positive way by saying, "Let's start over," when a disrespectful answer is given.[16] This gives them a chance to correct their behavior while letting them know what R-E-S-P-E-C-T means to you.

Cooperation. "Just as each of us has one body with many members, and these members do not all have the same function, so in Christ we who are many form one body, and each member belongs to all the others" (Romans 12:4–5). Our families, our faith, and our communities would not exist without cooperation—many different people coming together to accomplish their goals and dreams. Teamwork allows us to do more, be more, than we ever could alone. It can make work seem like fun. Through cooperation, we come to know others more intimately and develop a sense of belonging.

How can we foster a spirit of cooperation in our children? By playing cooperative games together in which everyone gets a turn and there is no clear winner. Just about any game can be made more cooperative with a slight tweaking of the rules. In a game of tag, give everyone the opportunity to be "it," and allow those who are out to be brought back into the game by other runners. If you're shooting baskets, let everyone have a turn and try to reach an ever-increasing number of points together. Working together in the home, making meals and doing the dishes side by side, encourages cooperation and shows how two (or more) sets of hands are better than one.

Unselfishness. My friend Kathy shared this story she heard in church that demonstrates a youngster's struggle with selfishness:

A mother was preparing pancakes for her sons, and the boys began to argue over who would get the first pancake. Their mother saw the opportunity for a moral lesson. "If Jesus were sitting here, He would say, 'Let my brother have the first pancake, I can wait.'"

The older son turned to his younger brother and said, "You be Jesus!"

Thinking of someone else first can be a difficult value to impart to kids because it's their nature to be so egocentric. Once again, doing the right thing ourselves—modeling sharing, caring, and helping—demonstrates the quality of unselfishness. Kids in this stage also learn to think beyond themselves through real-life opportunities to practice—in other words, by volunteering.

In the middle years, many kids discover what it means to be a volunteer through organizations like Scouts, or with school and church groups, by visiting nursing homes and helping with community projects such as park cleanups or food-pantry drives. One of the great things about volunteering is that there are so many people who need assistance and an infinite number of ways to help. If your children haven't experienced the glow that results from selfless service, you can help them get started.

"Charity begins at home," the old saying goes. Begin a long-term family volunteer recycling project with your children. After discussing why it's important to recycle (because the world God gave us has limited resources and He expects us to be good stewards of His creation) and going over which products to recycle, kids can help put the daily collectibles into the appropriate bag or bin at home. Our family goes together to deliver the full containers to the recycling pick-up point. If you'd rather try a one-time service project, Make a Difference Day—America's largest day of volunteering and community service—falls on the fourth Saturday in October. Check out www.usaweekend.com/diffday/index.html for project ideas and links to other volunteer organizations.

Before getting involved, try to match any volunteer opportunity to your family's available time and interests. Churches are often clearinghouses for volunteer activities. Our congregation asks families to participate in one big project each July. You might find us painting houses or building handicapped ramps for those in need. These big projects are in addition to weekly and monthly volunteer opportunities. Look under "Volunteer Services" in the yellow pages of your local telephone directory for other ideas. By getting involved, your children will learn that volunteering makes them feel good. Hopefully they will translate that understanding of unselfishness to others in their lives, like their siblings!

Discipline. The goal of discipline in the middle years is to encourage self-discipline in kids well in advance of those tumultuous teen years. Using consequences as tools of discipline works well now, mainly because kids care enough about some things that they can be taken away effectively as consequences of bad behavior. I'm only halfway kidding here. For example, when our son is caught playing his Game Boy outside of the minivan (he is only allowed to use it while traveling), taking it away for a period of time causes him distress on the same level as me having a root canal.

For consequences to be used correctly, for them to be valuable learning tools, there are several important requirements:

- Consequences must be practical and suited to the situation. If your child breaks a glass, it's more practical to ask her to help clean up the mess than to lecture and send her to her room.

- You must be prepared to follow through with a consequence you've established. Put some thought into it! A consequence should discipline the child not you.

- Youngsters at this age often need help making the connection between cause and effect. Talk through the action and consequence, and brainstorm about what he might have done instead.

I've heard macho dads say things like "It's a tough world out there, and the sooner kids learn that, the better off they'll be." My husband amended that to "Children need to learn that all decisions have consequences. Even though making a good ethical choice may be unpleasant now, it usually has positive consequences later, and vice versa." Some kids' actions don't require you to do anything for a consequence to be experienced. Examples of these natural consequences would be a child coming home hungry from school because he forgot to make his lunch or the anxiety he experiences because he put off practicing for the week's piano lesson. Resist the temptation to be a "fix it" mom and rush to shield your children from natural consequences. Instead, be supportive and encourage them to do a better job next time.

We discipline our children in hopes they will eventually learn to discipline themselves. Part of self-discipline is learning to make critical choices. With problem-solving tools in their pockets, kids' confidence will soar and they will be better equipped to choose what actions are worth the consequences. When your child comes to you with a problem, use these four steps to try to solve it:

Identify the real problem. Talk with your youngster until you get to the heart of the matter. If she starts by expressing an emotion, work back from that feeling until she figures out the actual problem.

Consider their options. Together, come up with as many solutions to the core problem as possible, no matter how outrageous.

Assess the possible consequences. For each solution, consider what the consequences could be. Let your child decide which ones she can live with and which ones she can't.

Choose it, plan it, do it. Have your child choose a solution from the possibilities, then develop a plan to put the solution into practice and do it!

Kids will continue to find discipline frustrating, so mothers must be ever mindful that our role is to provide the discipline children need without exasperating them to the point of further disobedience. This point was brought home to me by a comedienne's story about a time when her husband was out of town and her two girls engaged in a last-minute frenzy of energy and mischief right before bedtime. After sending the girls to their rooms, she rushed to her Bible to look up verses to quote about obeying and honoring your parents. She settled on Ephesians 6:1–3: "Children, obey your parents in the Lord, for this is right. 'Honor your father and mother'— which is the first commandment with a promise—'that it may go well with you and that you may enjoy long life on the earth.' " Then her eyes strayed down to the next verse: "Fathers, do not exasperate your children; instead, bring them up in the training and instruction of the Lord" (Ephesians 6:4). This bit of extra reading changed her plans of what the next step in discipline should be that night.

Modeling the virtues mentioned in the following verse is the surest way to communicate the importance of them to our children: "In everything set them an example by doing what is good. In your teaching show integrity, seriousness and soundness of speech that cannot be condemned" (Titus 2:7–8). Children don't arrive preprogrammed with morals and ethics. They emulate those around them. This is good news and bad news for me, because I know that I am not perfect myself. When I wonder why my older children constantly use their caustic wit on each other, I must admit that it's an unpleasant habit they've picked up from me. It's important for us to be disciplined in the examples we provide our kids—to think about what we as moms want to see in our children as they grow. By walking the walk, we provide a much more potent example of our beliefs than by just talking the talk.

Anne Frank wrote, "How wonderful it is that nobody need wait a single moment before starting to improve the world." You can start improving your little corner of the world today. Choose one of the virtues discussed here and focus on it during the next month with your child.

Mom's Moments

Do you have one standard of virtue for yourself and another for your child? Do you make him or her wear a seatbelt when you don't wear yours? Spend your money on things you don't value? Regardless of what you say, your actions may clearly communicate the message that rules are meant to be broken. Consider bringing your words and actions in line with your standards as a kind of self-improvement program—one that will allow you to live more authentically and honestly.

If you are struggling with issues of truthfulness in your own life, remember that you can always rely on the truth of God's Word. Keep a book of God's promises by your bedside as a reminder that there is someone trustworthy to whom you can turn.

Problem solving is one ability that does get better with age. Practice your own critical-thinking skills, focusing especially on the follow-through, which seems to get harder as we mature. Write down the steps toward resolution of a problem, and post them in a conspicuous place so you'll continue working toward a solution.

Can You Hear Me Now?

I have much to write to you,
but I do not want to use paper and ink.
Instead, I hope to visit you and talk with you face to face,
so that our joy may be complete.

2 JOHN 12

Have you ever played the telephone game, where everyone sits in a circle and one person whispers something to the next person, and the whispers continue around the circle? When the message reaches the last person, she announces what she heard, and it's compared with the original communiqué. The initial message and the final one *never* match; that's because being a good listener isn't easy. (As one of my friends jokes, "You didn't hear what I thought I said.")

When I hear the word *communicate*, I think of talking—

95

conveying my opinions, thoughts, and feelings. "Ears that hear and eyes that see—the Lord has made them both" (Proverbs 20:12). Have you ever sat down at the table with other people who talk incessantly, even to the point of talking over each other? If everyone is talking, no one is using those ears God gave us to listen. You might as well be speaking on your cell phone to someone in a no-service area!

How easy it is to forget that listening is more important than talking, particularly when it comes to children. In the middle years, kids are still trying to sort out their feelings and how to express them. Listening with our full attention allows us to demonstrate how much we care about what they have to say and validates their emotions. In contrast, what message do we send if we listen absentmindedly and give the same tired answer or miss much of what our child says while prematurely formulating a response?

Scripture cautions against the damage talk and the tongue can do, but it also provides many examples of leaders and apostles sharing information through conversation. "When the congregation was dismissed, many of the Jews and devout converts to Judaism followed Paul and Barnabas, who talked with them and urged them to continue in the grace of God" (Acts 13:43). Some kids are more communicative than others. One mom describes the difference in her sons' conversational skills this way:

> *My oldest son would come home from school in first, second, and third grade and I'd ask, "What did you do at school today?" "Nothing," he'd reply. So I would say, "Oh, come on. What did you do?" "Nothing." Two years*

later, my next son would start off with, "Well, first I hung up my coat." It would take forty-five minutes for him to tell me everything. "Six people had sack lunches, and then we did this, and this. . ."

Establishing a clear line of communication is key if you want to find out what's going on at school and inside their heads. In *What Did I Just Say!?!*, Denis Donovan and Deborah McIntyre suggest spending "five minutes a day alone, in private with each child *every single day* except when absolutely impossible."[17] Structuring your special time together according to the following guidelines will help you build open, honest, and trusting communication with your child.

- No interruptions including TV, radio, music, phone calls, beepers, little brothers barging in, or other disturbances of any kind.

- Games or other play should not compete with your conversation.

- This is your child's time to talk to you, not your time to talk to your child.

- Your youngster may tell you anything he or she cares to, as long as it's said respectfully.

- Your role is to understand and validate how your child feels about whatever he or she tells you.[18]

Some kids already put their ears to good use—when we least expect it. There are a couple of eavesdroppers in our house. One in particular likes to sit outside the door of a room from which he has been ushered to listen to my husband's and my private conversation (especially when the discussion is about a sibling). On the verbal side, my children are reluctant to let me know about their day at school, but are happy to tell me all about the "surprise" birthday gift my husband bought for me. According to my hubby, the kids have frequently "ratted me out" about a comment or minor event that was to be our little secret. He said the look on my face was quite interesting when these tidbits were revealed.

Children communicate with us in other ways besides verbal messages. In fact, only 10 percent of our communication is oral; the other 90 percent comes from the behaviors (or body language) that go with the words. To completely understand what children are saying, we need to read their nonverbal cues like posture, gestures, eye contact, and voice. Is your child slouched in defeat during the car ride home on report-card day? Does the tone of his voice communicate sadness even though he says, "I'm fine"?

We also communicate nonverbally with our children. As my son so eloquently puts it, "I know I'm really in trouble when you give me the 'death look.'" I certainly hope I have expressions or behaviors that convey my approval just as convincingly. The trouble comes not so much when our actions or body language match our words, but rather when they don't. Imagine how confused your youngster feels when you say, "I'm not mad that you broke the window. I know it was an accident," but then stomp off and slam the door to your room. Sending mixed messages tends to close the line of communication; it's much more important to say what you mean and mean what you say.

Social niceties also communicate the kind of person we are to those around us, which is another way of saying *manners matter*. "Why do we have to worry about manners?" my children whine. Indeed, manners today may seem very old-fashioned, very passé. I had the good fortune to have grown up in a traditional Southern home, where manners were second only to church on Sunday. My mother taught that you could tell the kind of person you were speaking with by the quality and depth of their manners. So imagine my dismay this past Mother's Day when my son insisted on cleaning his plate at the restaurant by scooping off every last bit of ketchup *with his finger.*

How important are manners in today's society? A friend of mine who is an employment counselor told me that employers invite potential candidates out to lunch specifically to check their manners. Now it's manners more than clothes that make the man or woman. Teaching manners during the middle years is particularly important because kids seem to regress significantly in this area during their teens. Prepare your child for life after home by requiring him or her to practice good manners, and not just at the table. A child cannot be expected to "mind his manners" when in public if you don't require the same behavior at home from all family members. If your family needs to move beyond please and thank you, choose one or two of these manners from Hermine Hartley's book, *Manners Matter*, to practice at a time:

- Don't ask how much someone weighs, if they are as rich (or poor) as everyone says they are, how much someone makes, or how much something cost.

- Ask permission before borrowing things, promptly return them to where you found them, and return them in the same or better condition than when you borrowed them.

- Never go to someone's house without first calling to ask if your visit would be welcome.

- Don't slam doors or run or throw things indoors.

- Don't open closed doors without knocking. Wait for permission to enter.

- Never chew with your mouth open or talk with food in your mouth.

- Try to excuse yourself from the table if blowing your nose is necessary.

- Don't reach across the table for food; ask for it to be passed to you.

- Avoid bad habits like: picking at any part of your body, spitting, passing gas, belching, sneezing, coughing, or yawning without covering your nose and mouth.[19]

It's tempting to leave the kids home when your family has been invited to a formal affair or plans to go out to dinner at a fancy restaurant (one where the food is actually served to you at your table). Moms need nice evenings out, but by insulating our children from these experiences, we deprive them of opportunities to practice their manners. The next time your family is invited to a special event, discuss ahead of time what will be expected, then bring the kids with you. At the very least, it will give the other guests something to talk about.

As you might have guessed from the finger-in-the-ketchup story, we still struggle with table manners at the Sumner house. But there is much more in the way of communication that can go on around the dinner table than practicing social niceties. Gathering together for a meal should be a relaxing experience—one that for many of us is on the endangered list. Even with all the lessons, practices, and meetings, we still try to break bread together as a family most days of the week. Spending *positive* time talking and laughing together gives me unique insights into how my kids think, how they feel, and what is important to them. As for myself, during mealtime I can look around the table and see just how blessed I really am.

The book of Proverbs says, "Better a meal of vegetables where there is love than a fattened calf with hatred" (Proverbs 15:17), so keep the discussion upbeat and affirming.

In the interest of harmony, we found it necessary to introduce three rules about our table talk:

1. Everyone gets a chance to talk—parents included.

2. No one may criticize anyone else (except for gentle reminders about manners).
3. Telling tales about others at the table is not allowed.

Jesus used the comfortable setting of the dinner table to impart wisdom and to minister to others. Whether He ate with tax collectors and other sinners (Matthew 9:10) or taught and talked with His disciples at His Last Supper, Jesus recognized the power of the camaraderie and comfort we feel sharing a meal around the table.

If your family tends to eat and run or the dinner table has become a battleground, make mealtime fun with new table traditions and conversation starters. If you're unsure how to start, begin on an encouraging note by telling a positive story about yourself, an anecdote that demonstrates one of the values discussed in the previous chapter. Then ask your family a thought-provoking question and give everyone an opportunity to answer. Here are a few to get you started:

- If you were elected president, what's the most important thing you would do for our country?

- When was the last time you laughed so hard you were out of breath? What was so funny?

- If you were to be marooned on a deserted island and could take only five things with you, what would they be?

- If you could change into another animal, what would it be?

- Think about your life so far. What are the five best things that have happened to you?

Some of our family friends go around the table and give everyone the chance to talk about their day. This mom remembers that the night before her youngest's first day of kindergarten, her older son (a big third grader) leaned across the table and said very seriously, "Okay, do you have any questions?"

For an affirming activity, designate one week a month as Family Appreciation Week. One person will be honored each day at dinnertime by all family members taking turns telling what they appreciate about him or her. No one can leave the table until everyone has given an appreciative comment. Another way to get kids talking is to go around the table and take turns describing the worst thing that happened that day, followed by the best or funniest.

Even if you can't get the family together regularly for a meal, stay in touch and keep the lines of communication open by holding regular family meetings. Family meetings allow kids to have more of a voice in household operations and give the entire family the chance to address everyday issues that come up, such as food, bedtimes, fights, vacations, and allowances. Some ground rules will help keep your meeting on track and focused on the cooperative mission of the group:

- No TV, radio, telephone, games, or other distractions allowed.

- Parents should provide leadership, but the rules of the meeting are the same for everyone.

- Only one person may hold the floor at any given time. Allow a suitable amount of time for airing a single issue or concern, but debate cannot continue ad nauseum.

- Next, the floor is opened for comments or a discussion of possible options. Anyone can speak, but only one at a time. If your kids don't volunteer, ask for their opinions.

- Agree upon a solution, and come up with a plan of action. Write it down and post the plan on the refrigerator if needed.

- Everyone should understand and accept that parents have the last word in difficult decisions.

- End the meeting with a display of affection and unity, like hugs all around.

- Hold another family meeting in a couple of weeks to review how the plan is working. All solutions should be considered experimental, so if yours isn't working, this is the time to reconsider other options.

I must admit that, after years of working in the corporate world, I have an aversion to meetings. Since my family is fortunate enough to eat and talk together regularly, we only use the family-meeting plan when something unusual or unusually serious comes up. When used sparingly, the meetings we do have generate interest and impact. Our last family meeting was called to formulate a solution to our kids' continual verbal sparring. It started off with my husband and me discussing how fed up we were with all the sniping and fighting. The children's first response was, "We won't do it anymore." Yeah, right! It took some time to get everyone talking about how the put-downs made them feel and to agree to a cease-fire.

What's the second best place, after the family table, to talk with kids? In your vehicle. Surveys show that one-third of all miles traveled by the typical adult or child involve driving to and from school, chauffeuring to children's activities or appointments, and running errands when children often must tag along. Who would have thought there are benefits to being trapped in the minivan? Children are a captive audience; they can't hide in the car. You also have fewer distractions than at home—none if you turn off TVs, radios, and cell phones. The minivan provides a comfortable, intimate environment where kids may share their deepest thoughts. Quiet youngsters may become chattier when they're not under the direct, scrutinizing gaze of a parent. Even uncomfortable subjects may be easier for you both to talk about when you are not sitting face-to-face. Driving in the car with your children's friends also yields interesting insights into their lives. Think of being confined together in the car as a license to eavesdrop, because kids often talk as if you're not there. Moms can find out the latest on what or who is "in" or "out."

As children grow, they naturally prefer to keep more of their thoughts and feelings private. That's hard for a hands-on mom like me. Frankly, it drives me nuts to ask about my child's day only to receive a monosyllabic response. I've had to learn to ask better questions like "What did you do in your favorite subject today?" instead of "How was school?" My kids also give me more information when I refrain from my usual habit of interrupting the flow of conversation with follow-up questions.

Being a good listener has other benefits; it encourages my family to listen when I have something to say. When Moses presented the Ten Commandments to the Israelites, he said, "These commandments that I give you today are to be upon your hearts. Impress them on your children. Talk about them when you sit at home and when you walk along the road, when you lie down and when you get up" (Deuteronomy 6:6–7). Keeping the lines of communication open allows us to pass along our values without the message getting garbled from outside interference. You won't have to keep asking, "Can you hear me now?" and that's good.

Mom's Moments

Communication in the minivan should not be limited to your children. My husband and I take every opportunity to run errands together while an older child baby-sits our kids. Driving around together gives us uninterrupted time to talk without little ears listening.

E-mail and telephone calls are no substitute for talking with someone face-to-face. Call a friend and arrange to meet over coffee or lunch and enjoy the gift of intimate conversation.

Have communications with your child become limited to orders and reprimands (what I refer to as drill-sergeant mode)? Remember to take five minutes every day just to listen to your child, then try extending that to another five or ten minutes of conversational give-and-take. Pay attention to the decibel level of your communications, as well. As one who lives in a rather raucous household, I've noticed that speaking loudly tends to put off those raised in quieter surroundings.

Rush Hour

A man can do nothing better than
to eat and drink and find satisfaction
in his work. This too, I see, is from the hand of God,
for without him, who can eat or find enjoyment?

ECCLESIASTES 2:24–25

Motherhood. Every mom I know agrees that mothering their children is the highest calling in their lives, but that doesn't mean that mothering is all we are called to do. If you already work outside the home, you are in good company. Studies show that over half of the moms with kids in the middle years have outside jobs in addition to their "home" work. This is a natural time for moms to reexamine their goals: personal, financial, and for their family. How best to meet those goals often leads us back into the workforce.

Why do so many moms decide to go back to work once their children are in school? Our new schedule affords us more flexibility. We need the money to keep pace with the growing needs of our family. Many of us enjoy the sense of satisfaction and affirmation we receive from working.

It's that last reason that causes so many questions in people's minds. If we feel that mothering is the highest calling in our lives, why can't moms be satisfied with that alone? Many moms do consider caring for their family the ultimate satisfaction, the height of contentment. Are these moms without ambition? No, their chosen work is to "be shepherds of God's flock that is under [their] care" (1 Peter 5:2). That's something everyone can appreciate and understand. I am constantly amazed, however, at the confusion surrounding why mothers would want to work outside the home.

In *Iron-Jawed Angels*, a movie about the suffragette movement, the main character, Alice Paul, is placed in a prison mental ward because of her pro-suffragette activities. The following discussion ensues between Alice and a doctor assessing her psychological state:

Doctor: *Explain yourself.*

Alice: *What needs to be explained? You want a place in the trades and professions to earn your bread. So do I. You want some means of self-expression. So do I.*

For most of us, the biggest obstacles to working or returning to work are the mixed feelings that result when our needs and others' expectations clash. Every mom deserves support and encouragement to satisfy her unique personality and aspirations, regardless of the work she chooses. When it comes to moms in the workplace, my attitude is the same as Alice's. What needs to be explained? A woman's work—all of it—is from the hand of God. He wants us to be satisfied in every area of our lives. One of my dear friends recently reentered the teaching profession as her youngest child was starting school because her ideal job became available. She was able to ease into the situation by starting at less than full-time. Her husband, who had recently sold his business, provided invaluable support by taking on the role of stay-at-home dad while going to night school. This was an opportunity for self-fulfillment that she couldn't pass up.

What does scripture have to say about a woman's work? I admit I find the portion of Proverbs 31 about "The Wife of Noble Character" intimidating. Read over this section with an eye toward what it tells us about the work in which this woman engages:

She selects wool and flax and works with eager hands. She is like the merchant ships, bringing her food from afar. She gets up while it is still dark; she provides food for her family and portions for her servant girls. She considers a field and buys it; out of her earnings she plants a vineyard. She sets about her work vigorously; her arms are strong for her tasks. She sees that her trading is profitable, and her lamp does not go out at night (Proverbs 31:13–18).

Wow! She is the Superwoman of the Old Testament. Who among us can live up to this ideal today? You would have to sew your family's clothes and get up before sunrise to have breakfast on the table and dinner in the Crock-Pot. Out of the considerable earnings from your home business, you would have sufficient cash to buy your own plot of land and pay all the household utility bills. In addition, you'd plant an orchard or garden on the new lot with your own two hands. Is anyone else feeling intimidated yet?

A speaker at a meeting I attended presented a new interpretation of this passage. Some scholars think that the Proverbs 31 woman is not *one* woman at all, but a composition of the admirable traits of several women. Whew! If you can get past feeling browbeaten by "The Wife of Noble Character," you'll notice that she works outside the home, cares for her family. . .and has household help! Looking at Proverbs 31 with new eyes leaves a mom's responsibilities and opportunities wide open.

Kids will have their own opinions about you going to work. They may feel fearful, disappointed, frustrated, angry, or even deserted. Perhaps it's time to have a family meeting to explain why you will be working, to allow family members to air their feelings about the change, and to let everyone know what to expect. Planning ahead will alleviate some anxiety about your family's new lifestyle and help everyone cope with the responsibilities of a different schedule.

Childcare requirements for working moms change dramatically once kids enter school. More and more churches, schools, and community centers offer after-school programs. A good after-school program provides competent, low-key supervision, while allowing kids the independence to choose their activities. In *The Working Mother's Guide to Life*, Linda Mason suggests the following things to look for in a program:

- A quiet place to do homework and quietly talk with a friend

- Active, outdoor play period at a minimum of thirty minutes

- A range of activities where children can pursue their interests

- A healthy snack

- Ratio of one staff member to ten to fifteen children

- Maximum group size of thirty in each room.[20]

It may be easier to find a baby-sitter to care for your child in your house (or in theirs) for the few hours until you get home. In the words of one of my friends, "A big factor was finding a sitter as close to work as possible. When my youngest was in kindergarten, she went to school in the building where I taught, so at lunch I could take her to the sitter's and then go back to work." In any case, childcare today remains at a premium, which means *you* may have to be more accommodating than originally planned. Monitor the quality of your child's care by asking him for feedback. Listen carefully to offhand comments your child makes—he may say more than just responses to your probing questions. Ask your neighbors or other parents with the same childcare arrangement how things are going. Finally, communicate regularly with your child's caregiver.

Many families with kids in the upper middle years allow their children to care for themselves at home before and after school. (Rely on your child's maturity level, not age, as the key factor in this decision.) If you are considering just such a "latchkey" arrangement, the American Academy of Pediatrics suggests you first discuss these issues with your child. Does he know his full name, address, and phone number, as well as the phone numbers of a neighbor and emergency services? Does he know your work information? Can he follow an established routine—know where he is supposed to be and what he is supposed to do (like check in by phone at designated times)? Does he know what to say or do if someone calls or comes to the door? Does your child know what to do in case of injury or an emergency like a fire? Kids should not be left alone unless they are comfortable with these situations.

One of my single-mom friends, who worked nights for a while, used this arrangement. A baby-sitter would stay at her house overnight and wake up her junior-high-age daughter before leaving at 6:00 a.m. It was then the daughter's responsibility to wake up her younger brother and get them both breakfast and off to school. This system allowed the mom to be home when the kids arrived after school and to enjoy dinnertime together. Now that my friend has switched to a daytime work schedule, she makes sure that her son (who usually gets home first due to his sister's after-school activities) has the house key in his bag and a snack ready. They keep all the telephone numbers handy, and her son calls her at work as soon as he gets home. Her children are not allowed to answer the telephone (unless they've screened the call and it's Mom or another family member) or the door without an adult in the house.

Whether you've been working since before your children arrived, just reentered the workforce, or devote your time and energy to managing your family and household, all moms must contend with the two busiest times of day: the morning rush and the evening crush. The fact that you also have to leave in the morning to go to work and return around dinnertime just exacerbates the situation. "Because of the Lord's great love we are not consumed, for his compassions never fail. They are new every morning; great is your faithfulness" (Lamentations 3:22–23). Thank goodness the Lord's compassion and mercy are new every day, because, despite our best efforts, mornings at our house are more mayhem than mellow. My husband and I constantly refine the morning routine in an attempt to promote a quiet and harmonious beginning to the day—or at the very least, to get everyone out the door on time. Here are our top five suggestions for slowing down the morning rush:

Divide morning jobs between family members. Making a list of all the things that must be done in your family's morning routine and assigning everyone a share allow you to work together as a team.

Get yourself and the kids up earlier than the bare-minimum time required for everyone to get ready. Murphy's Law says, "Anything that can go wrong will go wrong." We've all had mornings that prove Murphy's Law is just as unassailable as Einstein's theory of relativity. Building a time cushion into your morning makes allowances for the inevitable glitches; it also allows those of us who are not morning people to slowly get our motors running. On days when things go smoothly, use the extra time to read or pray together.

Do everything you can the night before. Being rushed in the morning makes everyone grouchy and starts the day on the wrong foot. Make sure all permission slips and forms are signed, homework is completed, and everything is packed in your child's book bag. Prepare lunches and put them in the refrigerator to be packed in the morning. Set out clothes to wear for the next day (no switching allowed). Set the break-fast table. Put each child's spelling list or other study material on his or her chair to look over while eating.

Just say no to distractions. We have a "no TV, video game, or computer before school" rule at our house. That way there's no battle to watch the end of a pro-gram or conquer the last enemy when it's time to leave. Our kids leave the house on a staggered sched-ule, so the one who's home longer in the morning uses this time to practice piano and play with his toys.

Always make time for breakfast. Your mother was right: It's the most important meal of the day. Keep a vari-ety of easy-to-eat finger foods on hand for days when you might have to eat in the car.

With family members returning home from a busy day, the evening crush presents another challenge. Everyone wants to talk about their day. There's homework and house-work to get done and dinner to prepare. Fatigue and the tension of transitioning from work and school to home and family contribute to the feeling of being crushed in the evening; we don't want to give the best of ourselves to our job and leave the tired mom for our kids. "He gives strength to the weary and increases the power of the weak" (Isaiah 40:29). It may help to take a moment to yourself and draw on the strength God offers by spending a few minutes alone when you first get home. Going to your room to put on some comfortable clothes gives you a moment of privacy and helps with the transition from working mode to mothering mode.

Kids need to shift gears, as well. During the first half hour of back-at-home time, turn on some soft music, turn off the telephone, and talk with your children about their day. Make sure everyone gets enough sleep by setting a reasonable bed-time and sticking to it (moms, too). If getting the kids to bed turns into a skirmish, insist that the TV be turned off half an hour before bedtime and enjoy a quiet activity together.

Here's how one busy elementary-school teacher with three girls of her own describes how she handles the first few hours after work:

> We have some time in the car when I'm picking everyone
> up so the girls can get out the big news of what happened
> during the day, the things they're just busting to tell me.
> When we get home, everyone goes to their own corners
> and gets homework started. If we can just have a little

downtime, a little separation, we can ease into the
evening. Sometimes I use this time to give special atten-
tion to our youngest, who is quite happy to sit with me
on the couch and look at a story for thirty minutes or so.

Dinner is the sticking point for my family. I used to be a good cook, I really did, but busy schedules and finicky eaters have taken all the fun out of the culinary arts. Now it's just a matter of getting something nutritious and filling on the table. To decrease evening stress, I plan easy dinners: sandwiches, spaghetti, and meat on the grill. Even though it's difficult to have leftovers with a six-foot-three-inch husband and three growing children, making enough to put a few extra servings in sealable plastic containers gives those who come home late a quick and easy meal.

Dinner tips contributed by other moms include cooking main dishes on the weekend and refrigerating or freezing them to eat during the week. This way, whoever gets home first can start warming up the meal. You'll also eat more nutritiously than picking up fast food because everyone is starving. Another mom has a meal plan for each week when certain dinners are scheduled for specific nights. For example, Wednesday night is tacos and Friday night they eat pizza. No more angst over what to serve!

Moms have more job options available to them than ever before. Progressive employers make it easier for moms to satisfy their need to work outside the home *and* to fulfill their family obligations with flextime, part-time, and telecommuting arrangements. Flextime allows staff to begin work very early so they can leave and be home when their kids return from school. Part-timers work a variety of hours and days, and with a job-share schedule, one position is shared by two people. My first job after having children was a telecommuting position as a freelance writer. Given the rural area in which we live, this arrangement has been a blessing, like an answer to the psalmist's prayer: "May the favor of the Lord our God rest upon us; establish the work of our hands for us—yes, establish the work of our hands" (Psalm 90:17). God does provide!

I like to refer to working from home as the best of all worlds and the worst of all worlds. The best is easy to see. Flexible hours, availability to my children, no commute, no parking hassles, no pantyhose! However, working from home presents its own special challenges, the biggest of which is that, well, you're home. Even if your kids are in school, there's always laundry, dishes, and clutter calling to you. Deadlines can't be put on hold for sick kids or summer vacation. Friends, family, and associates rarely equate a home business with a "real" job, so they feel free to call or drop by and ask for help with a problem or project or for company on a shopping trip (actually, this goes under both the pluses and minuses columns).

Working at home presents challenges above and beyond scheduling. You have to be organized, disciplined, and willing to take risks; but as a side benefit, your children see you doing a job you enjoy and being there for them. How do I manage my home business?

Work with my daily rhythm. My most productive time of day is in the morning, so even with the dishes on the counter, the bed unmade, and the laundry basket overflowing, I sit down and work conscientiously for a few hours before doing anything else. Errands, phone calls, and chores are reserved for less productive afternoon and evening hours, times when interruptions are frequent (and welcome). You may focus more clearly in the afternoon or evening. Try to build a schedule that accommodates your own daily rhythm.

Do some work every day. There certainly are days when I don't feel like chaining myself to the computer to write, but that doesn't mean I don't work. I can set up or conduct interviews, read through resource material, write an outline, or look up quotations. My goal is to accomplish something toward the completion of a current project each and every day.

Continue to be as professional and organized as you can be. Keep clear, complete records. This is easier said than done. When you are self-employed, a whole new set of paperwork is required: receipts for expenses, pay stubs, invoices for the cost of goods you plan to sell, invoices for services you've provided, estimated tax payment vouchers. Having your own space designated specifically for your home business goes a long way toward containing the clutter and keeping some semblance of order.

Do you remember a commercial for a phone company where a woman with a home business is conducting an interview from her house in her pajamas and fuzzy slippers? I'm afraid to say I've done worse. If videophones ever really make it, I could be in big trouble! My clothing may not comply with an office dress code, but I do make sure that I am always well prepared for telephone meetings and that my correspondence and other work is completed in a timely and professional manner.

Turn down requests to help out if they interfere with a deadline. It's so easy to fall into the trap of saying yes when someone calls and needs a replacement room mother because the original one moved away or to help at the concession stand when it's shorthanded. I have to remind myself that my deadlines are no less important simply because I don't go to work in an office. If I don't respect my own need for work time, who else will?

Regardless of our chosen professions, the Lord provides ample work for a mom's hands. "For he is our God and we are the people of his pasture, the flock under his care" (Psalm 95:7). Whatever job you find fulfilling—homemaker, teacher, consultant, banker, accountant, writer, artist—take your cue from the Proverbs 31 woman and go for it *vigorously*. The door is open for you to choose the work that satisfies your family's needs as well as your own.

Mom's Moments

Daily and weekly family rituals become even more important when work separates you from your children. Use special times like walks after dinner, family video nights, and special weekend breakfasts to reconnect and strengthen your relationships.

You will have to make more choices about how your time away from work is spent, but don't abandon all of your interests. Maintain your own identity by holding on to a favorite hobby or activity.

Be sure that the level of achievement you expect from yourself is not too high. Women today can have it all, just not necessarily all at the same time. Don't give up today while reaching for tomorrow.

Slave Labor

Whatever you do, work at it with all your heart,
as working for the Lord, not for men,
since you know that you will receive an inheritance from
the Lord as a reward. It is the Lord Christ you are serving.

COLOSSIANS 3:23–24

I am a firm believer in child labor—the kind kids perform because it is their contribution as part of a family. That's not to say I don't often feel it would be a lot easier just to do things myself. Last week I'd put in my third request for my son to empty his one-third portion of the clean dishes from the dishwasher so that I could load the dirty ones. I guess the third time really is the charm, because he got up off the couch and came zooming into my office on his way to the kitchen. Somehow he forgot about the filing cabinet that has been sitting just inside the door for the past eight years. As you would expect, the ensuing collision caused him more damage than the cabinet. Off to the emergency room we went to care for his broken toe. While we were waiting in X-ray, I told him, "If you didn't want to do your chores, you didn't have to break a bone to get my attention!"

Helping with chores teaches kids respect for others and their property; it equips them to eventually live on their own. "Train a child in the way he should go, and when he is old he will not turn from it" (Proverbs 22:6). As those on whose shoulders the main responsibility for housework usually falls, we also do ourselves a disservice if we fail to share the family workload. Youngsters in the middle years can help more around the house than the average preschooler. If you're not sure what age-appropriate tasks to assign your child, here's a list of chore possibilities for the middle years:

Put away clean laundry	Make the bed and tidy room
Run the vacuum cleaner	Water the plants and weed
Take out the trash	the garden
Set the table	Clear the table
Feed and water the pets	Sweep the floor and sidewalk
Help with dishes	

For me, finding chores is the easy part. Deciding who should do what and getting them to do it—now that's difficult. My children put up less of a fight as long as they know that everyone has something to do. Our family often works together to reinforce that everyone's contribution is valuable, as well as to help kids learn new tasks. "Diligent hands will rule, but laziness ends in slave labor" (Proverbs 12:24). They may complain about being used as "slave labor," but they do not slave alone. We use a chore chart and rotate responsibilities weekly. If they hate the job they have, they know it will last for only one week. The kids understand their jobs, what's expected of them, and what will happen if the work isn't done. (There are those consequences again.)

Beyond chores, instituting a few basic rules helps keep housework under control. This set of house rules was hanging on the wall of a beach house we once rented:

- If you got it out, put it back.
- If you're finished with it, put it away.
- If you wore it, hang it up.
- If you spilled it, clean it up.
- If you help me, I'll help you.

Some moms are reluctant to ask their children to help around the house for various reasons:

"I'm a stay-at-home mom. It's my job to make sure that all the housework is done and done well." This mom believes that she only fulfills her role if she takes care of everything herself. Children learn to value the work it takes to run a household if they, too, have the chance to participate.

"If my kids do a chore, I usually just have to go back and redo it to my satisfaction anyway." God is more interested in our availability than our ability. It's only through practice that anyone becomes proficient at a new skill. If we don't take the time to teach kids how to do chores then accept imperfection as they try and try again, they will not develop the confidence to be self-sufficient.

"My youngsters are so busy with schoolwork and extracurricular activities that it doesn't seem fair to burden them with household responsibilities, too." Kids in this household learn that work and fun are more important than being a family team. Will they be prepared for the responsibilities of adulthood when they move away from home?

If your children fulfill their household responsibilities reluctantly or not at all, offer them choices of jobs they prefer. Try using a timer and have everyone work as hard as they can for thirty minutes, or play your child's favorite lively CD. Helping around the house instills the value of service and discourages an attitude of "I'm too good for that job." We should all follow the example Jesus set at the Last Supper where He took on the lowly job of washing and drying the disciples' feet.

When he had finished washing their feet, he put on his clothes and returned to his place. "Do you understand what I have done for you?" he asked them. "You call me 'Teacher' and 'Lord,' and rightly so, for that is what I am. Now that I, your Lord and Teacher, have washed your feet, you also should wash one another's feet. I have set you an example that you should do as I have done

*for you. I tell you the truth, no servant is greater than
his master. . . . Now that you know these things, you
will be blessed if you do them" (John 13:12–17).*

My mother and father are the children of parents who
grew up in the Depression. My grandparents made sure that
money-management skills and the benefits of saving were
deeply ingrained in their kids. Through the trickle-down
effect, my parents transferred these values to me; but a funny
thing happened with my generation. Either we rejected their
teaching or we were comfortable enough that the ability to save
or to budget didn't seem necessary. As a result, most moms I
speak with do not give their kids an allowance; instead, they
give their kids money as needed. They do agree that this
method probably is not best for children in the long run.

*We didn't give our children allowances and that's one
thing we've regretted. They always helped out around the
house, and we would just give them money when something would come up and they needed cash. Now that our
children are older, they don't seem to have the money-
management skills we hope for. My husband and I grew
up receiving an allowance, so I'm not really sure why we
didn't continue the practice with our kids. I guess I never
wanted an allowance to be a carrot I was dangling in
front of them, or something held over their heads.*

There are two main schools of thought about weekly
allowances: earned allowances and discretionary allowances.

Earned allowance. This system simulates life in the real world, where work is rewarded with money. Your child cannot count on an allowance each week unless he has completed his agreed-upon chores. Moms should sit down with their kids and clearly discuss what needs to be accomplished to earn the stated allowance. One positive aspect of earned allowances is that money is a powerful inducement, even for kids in the middle years. On the negative side, if you have a child who isn't interested in cash, he might choose to blow off his chores and accept the reduction in spending money.

Discretionary allowance. Parents who give allowances independent of chores do so to teach children the importance of working together, because chores are a responsibility that goes along with being a family member. In this case, you need to decide in advance on the consequences of not doing chores and communicate them to your kids. What if your children could care less about the spirit of family cooperation and a smoothly running household? Take time to praise and congratulate them for jobs well done. In extreme circumstances, add a little extra pressure by employing a reasonable consequence. For example, you could say, "The TV stays off until you have set the table and put water in the glasses."

My husband, the banker, helped me come up with this exhaustive list of advantages for giving allowances, no matter which system you use:

- saves Mom and Dad from constantly being asked for money
- teaches children how to set priorities for spending money (elementary budgeting)
- teaches the real cost of things
- provides experience practicing how to save
- begins a habit of giving to others or tithing at church
- gives youngsters the chance to become better consumers and more discriminating about advertising

As you can see by this story, some kids need more help with budgeting than others, and an allowance gives them extra chances to practice.

When my boys were twelve and fourteen, they went off to basketball camp in the summer. We gave them fifty dollars each spending money for pop, pizza, and whatnot. When we went to pick them up, the oldest came home with forty dollars. His younger brother approached my husband and said, "Dad, I owe that kid over there five dollars." He had spent everything we'd given him and asked a stranger for a five-dollar loan!

When kids buy their own goodies and toys, they develop a more realistic appreciation for how much things cost, as illustrated by this story:

A mom's daughter always wanted to stop at the local convenience store to get a drink after dance class. The mother rarely carried much cash around, so she was always telling her daughter, "I don't have any money on me." One day the daughter said, "Well, my third-grade teacher must be really rich, because she brings a Coke to class with her every morning!"

The next decision is how much to give or how much your child can earn. The amount of an allowance should be affordable for parents (consider how many times you have to multiply that amount for each child) and dependent on your child's age and what she will be expected to pay for. Plan ahead so that you can increase the allowance and what it should cover in small amounts each year. I also feel that an allowance should not be so large that a child has all the money she desires. This strategy gives her an incentive to save and to occasionally perform extra tasks to earn additional money.

Proverbs 13:11 reveals a great truth to impress on children: "He who gathers money little by little makes it grow." Being a banking family, we require our kids to put a portion of each allowance (one-third) into a savings account, which they are not to touch without very good reason before age sixteen. This means, in setting an allowance, we started with how much each child should have in spending money, then added on the necessary amount to be put in savings. Much to our surprise, we have a couple of supersavers in our family who have asked for the portion of every allowance going into savings to be increased to one-half.

Tithing or giving are important principles in many families and prevalent in scripture. "Honor the LORD with your wealth" (Proverbs 3:9). However, with money tight for so many families, it's hard to establish a discipline of giving. Instead of handing your child a quarter on Sunday morning to take to Sunday school, increase his allowance by that amount. By making it his responsibility now, you'll be laying the foundation for a willing spirit of giving later.

Allowances give kids the opportunity to make their own buying decisions—for better or for worse. One of our children's first lessons in consumer advertising came in the form of an airplane he saw advertised on TV. It seemed like a lot to pay for such a toy, but my son would not be dissuaded. He diligently saved his money, and one day we made the trip to the toy store. My son wanted to try out the plane as soon as we got home. It flew about ten feet and both of the wings promptly fell off! We ended up getting a refund, but the lesson he learned was worth much more—advertisements are designed to make products look bigger, faster, and better than they usually are. No matter how many times I might have told him that the picture looked too good to be true, finding the truth out for himself educated my son in ways my words could not.

I recently spoke with a mom who complained about her adult son's friends and how they expect things to be given to them and done for them but never want to work in return. She said, "I think it's because they were pampered all their lives. Their parents never asked them to work at home, so now they don't really have a clue of how to put in an honest day's work for an honest wage." When parents don't model and encourage a solid work ethic, they produce kids who struggle with jobs and relationships. Children should not leave home expecting to start life on their own at the same socioeconomic level they left while in their parents' care. It likely took them twenty or thirty years of hard work to get where they are today. Sending kids off with the idea that they can immediately move into a choice job, home, vehicle, and lifestyle sets them up for dissatisfaction and, worse, failure.

In *Blue Monday*, Robert Eisenberger writes:

> *One of the reasons the United States became a great economic power was, quite simply, the industriousness of its people. . . . As America became affluent, a preoccupation with leisure began to replace traditional work values, making managers, workers, and students less willing to undergo the self-denial required to achieve long-term goals. Society's emphasis on getting ahead by hard work disappeared before most of today's Americans were born. More than ever before, Americans view school and work as an unpleasant interlude in their relaxation and entertainment, to be gotten out of the way with a minimum of effort.*[21]

At work as in life, " 'Whoever wants to become great among you must be your servant, and whoever wants to be first must be your slave—just as the Son of Man did not come to be served, but to serve, and to give his life as a ransom for many' " (Matthew 20:26–28). What attitude do you exhibit for your children about work in the home or out? Are you willing to start at the bottom in a new endeavor? Do you hurry to complete a task even if the result is inaccurate or sloppy? Do you whine and complain or find joy and satisfaction in a job well done?

Instilling a positive work ethic in your youngster is one

of the most important gifts a mom can give, but all the chore charts and allowances in the world won't help if you are not dedicated to doing the best *you* can at whatever job you undertake. "Whatever you do, work at it with all your heart, as working for the Lord" (Colossians 3:23). Let your child see your willingness to be a servant following Jesus' example—to give a job your all, whether the work is white-collar, blue-collar, or T-shirt and Lycra shorts (my work uniform of choice). Rewarding children for hard work, in whatever way you see fit, also helps strengthen their work ethic, so that one day they can hear, "Well done, good and faithful servant!"

Mom's Moments

How can chores enrich your life? Take the time to pray for those for whom you are working. When you replace the batteries in the latest electronic toy, pray for its owner. As you wash dishes, pray for those who enjoyed the meal and ask the Lord to continue to provide the "daily bread."

Don't try to do all the work yourself. Remember, having a share of the household responsibilities is good for kids. What tasks can you turn over to them this week?

Money management is an issue for many moms. Dedicate this month to buying only the essentials and find out how much you really don't need.

"We're All Fruit?"

*Therefore, as we have opportunity, let us do good to all people,
especially to those who belong to the family of believers.*

GALATIANS 6:10

One of the funniest movies I've seen in recent years is *My
Big Fat Greek Wedding.* In the story, the daughter of an
Orthodox Greek family falls in love with the son of a reserved
New England family. The father of the bride in the story has
a funny habit of giving people the Greek root of words in the
English language. During his toast at the wedding reception,
the father talks about the Greek origins of the last names of
the bride and groom. One surname means "apples" and the
other "oranges." The father says, "We have apples and oranges.
We're all different, but in the end, we're all fruit." That's the
way I think of our family, because we're all pretty fruity!

There should be room for all different kinds of people in a family. It's the combination of all the different "flavors" that makes each family unique.

The concept of family is important in the Bible, as evidenced by all those extensive genealogies sprinkled throughout. In biblical times, families typically lived together in large extended groups of three or more generations (plus any servants living with them) or in an even larger circle of relatives bonded by common ancestry. The nuclear family with only Mom, Dad, and the kids is a relatively recent phenomenon. Today families come in all shapes, sizes, and flavors. Many parents and children face the challenges of divorce, single-parenthood, stepfamilies, and blended families.

One mom describes her emotions during a recent divorce. "You feel like such a failure when your marriage falls apart. I think that was the hardest thing for me to have to deal with, because I'd never failed at anything important in my life before. It was a humbling experience that really made me stop and think about how I look at other people." Christians divorce at virtually the same rate as the rest of society but often have more difficulty coping in the aftermath. Besides emotional and financial impact, they also must face the loss on a spiritual level.

Children's responses to divorce vary. They may be angry with you and go through a period of mourning over the loss of their family as they knew it. Kids can feel angry at themselves or feel they are somehow to blame for the breakup. Almost all youngsters experience anxiety or fear about what the future will hold. In their book *What about the Kids?* Judith Wallerstein and Sandra Blakeslee suggest establishing structure and routines to help kids from separated or divorced homes feel settled and safe:

- Explain why you will be going back to work or working longer hours (to provide for their needs).

- Maintain regular schedules, like bedtime, and rituals such as nighttime stories and kisses good-bye in the morning.

- Avoid turning over the rearing of younger children to an older sibling. They do not have the wisdom, patience, or tolerance to raise small children on their own.

- House rules should be clear and firm.

- Think of activities or treats that you can arrange together to lighten up this difficult time.[22]

Divorce transforms the lives of everyone in your family, but children weather the storm of divorce best when ex-spouses continue to work together in parenting and are willing to make compromises for the sake of their kids.

Here is a tale of two families who share their experiences with divorce, single-motherhood, and blended family life. With different outcomes and lifestyles, their stories remain united by a common thread: *always pursuing the best for their children in the midst of difficult circumstances.* The first mom has a "yours, mine, and ours" household and a close amicable relationship with her ex-husband:

I feel we are all very fortunate that my ex and I live in close proximity to each other. It really helps that the boys see their dad every day. We have a good working relationship. He picks them up from school, and we take turns with dinner. They stay overnight at their dad's house at least two nights a week. He takes them to school on those mornings and their stepmom does what she can to help. She was even out on the ball field one evening with a flashlight helping my youngest son look for his favorite rock! I know that I can count on her.

My new husband and I, and my ex and his wife, spend time every day communicating and coordinating our schedules. I promised myself when we got divorced that I would never play one parent against the other, so we get along. We have to, or else it wouldn't be fair to the kids. I'm also lucky my parents and immediate family live nearby; that's been a godsend with everything that has gone on. They were such a big emotional help and a physical help, too, because my mom baby-sat all three of my children when they were younger. I do get frustrated and upset with my ex-husband at times, but I've decided to keep my feelings in check and not fight. I want my kids to be able to honestly tell people who find out they're from a divorced family, "No, my parents didn't fight. They always got along." We also still maintain close ties with each other's families because of the boys.

Working out the relationship with my husband's

*daughter from his first marriage was a little more diffi-
cult because she lives some distance away and is only
with us every other weekend and every other week during the summer. I've let my stepdaughter's mom know
that "I want to help you raise your daughter, but I'm
never going to try to take your place." We're just all here
to support the kids. I've told our children that they're
very lucky because they have four parents who care very
deeply for them—who are available to do what we can
to help see them through life. No matter what comes up
in our children's lives, there will always be someone they
can talk to.*

As in this mom's story, a new stepfamily can provide an
enriching experience for all family members. However,
remarried parents should expect kids to have concerns like
adjusting to new rules and coping with feelings of divided
loyalty. Unreasonable expectations, such as having a household that immediately runs smoothly or stepchildren who
instantaneously develop close, loving relationships with their
new stepparent, can lengthen the time of transition and create hard feelings in the process.

Ron Deal recommends integrating stepfamilies with a
"Crock-Pot cooking style":

*Stepfamilies choosing this style understand that time
and low heat make for an effective combination.
Ingredients are thrown together in the same pot, but
each is left intact, giving affirmation to its unique ori-
gin and characteristics. Stepfamilies need time to adjust*

*to new living conditions, new parenting styles, rules,
and responsibilities. Cooking with low heat refers to
your gradual, intentional efforts to bring the parts
together. It is working smarter, not harder.*[23]

Stepfamily relationships go through stages, just like
someone dealing with grief or an addiction. By allowing
family members the time they need to accept and understand
one another, the new family can arrive at a level of stability
and respect that works for all.

This second story is of a woman who lived through a
divorce she contested and now is a single mom raising her
two children:

*The best thing I did for the kids when we divorced was
to let them feel everything they needed to feel. I was
very up front with my children and told them that I
still loved their daddy and I was going to do everything
possible to make our family whole again. At the time of
our separation, I didn't live close to my own family, so
my church family became my family. I relied upon them
for wisdom and strength when I couldn't see clearly. My
friends let me ask a million times, "Why?" and tell them
again and again that this was not something I wanted.*

*The biggest lesson God taught me was to be open to
asking for help. I learned that I could need someone, and
that was okay. After the divorce, we moved back to where
my family lived so I could go back to school. It was the
best thing I ever did, but it was the hardest decision to
make. There were times I had to sell belongings just*

to pay the utilities. I wasn't in control of my situation, and I had to let people help. It was hard to accept that bag of groceries even though there was no food in the refriger-ator. It was a lesson for my children, too—to come home and flip the light switch and there were no lights because I hadn't been able to pay the electric bill.

The kids saw how difficult things were for us but that we could make it through and be all right. It started new traditions for us like praying together. I had always prayed by myself but never really included the kids. It was wonderful to hear their simple heartfelt prayers. When we prayed together at night, my oldest son once said, "Mom, you know, if this hadn't happened, you prob-ably wouldn't be as close to the Lord as you are now. You probably wouldn't know Him the way you do."

The experience of being a single mom is actually more common than being a stepmom; over one-fourth of all chil-dren in the United States live with only one parent. As the second mom's story shows, being a single parent can be among the most challenging of family arrangements. Most single moms work outside the home, and their responsibilities do not stop at the end of the workday. They are prone to feelings of helplessness and hopelessness resulting from severe burnout, not to mention a nonexistent social life. The good news is that children are adaptable. Single mothers don't have to have all the answers; their kids just need to know they aren't alone with their feelings. To accommodate new financial pressures, moms may need to adjust their expectations of what children need in order to be happy, and children often must assume new responsibilities and adjust to new schedules. Single moms really need other sources of support to help them cope with the endless requirements of caring for a family.

Regardless of your marital status, sharing the joys and responsibilities of raising a child makes mothering more enjoyable and less overwhelming for all moms. Your child's father is a natural parenting partner, but there can be others. Members of the extended support network we create for our kids can range from grandparents and other relatives to close family friends. As one mom says, "We are so fortunate that our kids always *want* their grandparents to stay with them when my husband and I have to go out of town." Children gain many advantages through close relationships with their grandmothers and grandfathers—love is the first and foremost. Author Pearl Buck wrote, "The lack of emotional security of our American young people is due. . .to their isolation from the larger family unit. [A child] needs to feel himself one in a world of kinfolk, persons of variety in age and temperament, and yet allied to himself by an indissoluble bond which he cannot break if he could, for nature has welded him into it before he was born."

Including grandparents in our extended family multiplies a child's opportunities to experience love and acceptance. Grandparents offer an emotional safety net when parents falter, and they have a magical ingredient that parents often lack—time. In addition to love, there are four other important things grandparents give their grandchildren:

Family culture. Grandparents reinforce family traditions and make them seem like fun instead of a chore.

Sense of history. Grandparents extend the family's collective memory and relate stories that don't seem like history lessons.

Second opinions. Grandma or Grandpa often lends another ear when a child feels uncomfortable talking to Mom or Dad.

Special perspective. Grandparents help kids see their own parents as human when they share stories about Mom and Dad as kids.

Encourage kids and grandparents to spend one-on-one time together so their relationship can develop without interference. Keep your children on the sidelines of any conflict between adults in your extended family. Youngsters shouldn't have to choose between you because of adult disagreements. Don't allow differences to deprive them of an important source of love and support. Sometimes grandparents can forget what it was like to be or raise a child. They may have unrealistic expectations of their grandchildren— and their grandchildren's parents, too! However, they also can impart some of the wisdom that comes from experience. They can share the fears they had as parents and, in the process, help dispel our own. Making room for grandparents in your extended family is not always easy, but in many ways they can be a family's most valuable resource.

The saying "It takes a village to raise a child" has become cliché, but children can never have too much love and support in their lives. Many women include other moms as part of their extended family circle. Living next door or in the same neighborhood is very helpful in these kinds of relationships. My friend Kathy relates, "I was part of a play group when my children were very young, and we continued that group for many years. I knew that anytime I had an emergency, I could call any one of those mothers and ask for help. It's so nice to have a buddy system for all the daily carpooling, too. We all need help coordinating our children's lives."

The Old Testament emphasizes the physical family, while "family" in the New Testament also means the church or the Christian community. Paul wrote, "I pray that you, being rooted and established in love, may have power, together. . .to grasp how wide and long and high and deep is the love of Christ, and to know this love that surpasses knowledge—that you may be filled to the measure of all the fullness of God" (Ephesians 3:17–19). As children of the same Father, we have an obligation to help those in His family as we would a sister or brother. Just as the single mom in the earlier story relied on her church family to see her through difficult times, our common identity also gives us the opportunity to reach out for support from the members of God's extended family when we are in need.

Mom's Moments

Make a list of the people you know you can count on as extended family. If your list is too short, work on developing other relationships to build your own parenting network.

Do you know another mom who could use the support of a good friend? Reach out in love to another member of God's family, whether or not she is a member of your community of faith.

The Lord is the architect of your life, but you are the general contractor. Join a group or pursue an interest where you can make some new acquaintances.

Creatures of Habit

Put to death, therefore,
whatever belongs to your earthly nature. . . .
You used to walk in [evil] ways, in the life you once lived.
But now you must rid yourselves of all such [vices].

COLOSSIANS 3:5, 7–8

I like a large mug of hot tea in the morning, just like my grandmother used to make—except it's decaf. I usually play a game of spider solitaire on the computer before starting to work. I also eat lunch right at twelve o'clock, always put my dirty clothes in the clothes basket, and have to sleep on my side. Our lives are made up of habits. The daily ones have become so routine that they can be hard to identify. If a habit is defined as an activity that is done frequently, automatically, and is difficult to stop, then most of what we do involves habitual behavior. Putting it that way makes habits sound *bad*, but most of our habits are good ones, or at least neutral: brushing our teeth regularly, checking on the kids before going to bed, washing fruit before eating it, exercising regularly. (Okay, that last one is more wishful thinking than habit.) Still, it's those bad habits that make the news and lurk in the back of our minds.

An old saying warns:

Watch your thoughts, for they become your words
Watch your words, for they become your actions
Watch your actions, for they become your habits
Watch your habits, for they become your character
Watch your character, for it becomes your destiny.

—Unknown

We often make new habits without seeming to notice, but changing an established habit requires intentional effort. According to Elisa Morgan, "The best way to break a habit is to undo what you did. Layer by layer, we must unlearn what we learned. Ask yourself: What good is this habit doing me? Why did I build this habit in the first place? What has this habit taught me about myself?"[24] Sometimes breaking an old habit and building a new one go hand in hand. Studies show that it takes twenty-one days to establish a new habit by constructing a basic pattern and repeating it over and over again. All this behavioral science is helpful for moms who want to break a shopaholic habit or begin a habit of healthy eating. However, this type of self-analysis does not work as well on my seven-year-old, who chews his fingernails.

Just like adults, children have good and bad habits. During the middle years, kids exhibit what psychologists call *tensional outlets*—habits developed as soothing mechanisms to release tension. Moms tell me their youngsters engaged in hair twirling, fuzz picking, pencil- or pen-cap gnawing, and shirt chewing. You may have noticed some of these behaviors in the early years. Youngsters revisit old calming habits as they deal with the stresses of growing up, but most of these disappear on their own over time. For the annoying, die-hard habits (like chewing with your mouth open), you may be less inclined to wait it out. We've had some success with the three Rs:

Recognition. Once a habit becomes firmly entrenched, you don't even realize you're doing it. Pointing out the behavior to your child and talking about why it's improper or offensive gets him to think more about his actions.

Reminders. Most kids do not have the internal discipline to stop a behavior simply because you ask them to. Frequent, gentle reminders are needed to reinforce a changing habit.

Rewards. Younger children still may respond to traditional techniques like sticker charts or crossing days off of a calendar, especially if positive performance is linked to some tangible reward. Loads of praise also provides necessary encouragement. Celebrate by going out for a special treat once a child has kicked the habit.

We live in the information age—for all its pros and cons, technology is here to stay. One of the most prominent and controversial habits concerns the amount of time kids should spend engaged with their TV, computer, or video games. A family down the street from us instituted a "no TV" policy in their home several years ago. This is easier in our rural community than in others, because without an antenna on the house (not to mention cable or satellite connections), receiving any stations is difficult. They do have a TV and DVD player in the home so everyone can watch parent-approved movies. Unfortunately, TV time is a battle we fight constantly in our home, partly because I am somewhat of a TV addict.

I still can remember, as a child, that they interrupted *Flipper* on our black-and-white set to inform the country that President Kennedy had been shot. My parents woke my sister and me up in the middle of the night so we could watch, mesmerized, the lunar landings and men walking on the moon. I went through a soap-opera phase and a game-show obsession (thankfully, I broke both habits). I've watched some of the defining moments in current history on the TV, such as the day I tuned in to watch the morning news just in time to see the first World Trade Center building collapse.

My family's problem is not so much that we want to watch TV all the time, but that we all like to watch different shows at different times. I like to watch movies and shows on the History Channel, Discovery Channel, and A&E. My husband likes to watch sports. My sons like Cartoon Network (which my husband and I sneak in to watch with them), and my daughter watches *Cosby Show* and other teenage sitcoms on Disney. Between the five of us, the TV would need to be on all afternoon and evening to catch everything we would like to see. That presents a big problem, because TV is addicting. It's difficult to walk through a room and not stop to see what's happening on the screen. Stopping leads to sitting down, and sitting down leads to ignoring whatever you were supposed to be doing until the show is over.

I don't think I could ever completely get rid of the TV the way some families have, and I wouldn't want to. Kids will hear about the things other children watch, even if the TV is persona non grata in your home. I prefer to monitor and limit TV viewing and to use it as a tool to teach our kids the skills they need to put what they see and hear in perspective. The average middle-years child watches almost twenty-two hours of television a week. According to Michael Medved and Diane Medved in their book *Saving Childhood*, "The impact of this invasion is profound—redefining norms, creating slang terms, presenting the negative but not the positive side of reality with the daily news."[25] Clearly this absorption with media is part of our nature. Sadly, as the amount of time we spend with media increases, the quality of available material is declining rapidly. This partial list of the negative aspects of television viewing on children points out the need for vigilance and control on the part of parents. Studies show that TV tends to make kids

- more aggressive and more insensitive to another's sadness and pain

- prematurely knowledgeable about "adult" topics like crude language and sexuality

- have declining attention spans

- less inclined and able to entertain themselves

- more materialistic but less able to wait for what they want

- overweight and out of shape

- dissatisfied with their own lives

- confused about moral and spiritual values

What's a former TV junkie to do? One of my friends submits,

> *TV and electronic media are good things to use as bargaining chips, as in, "You may not get on the computer until you've finished your homework and your chores. Then feel free to do whatever you'd like." I am wishing, now that my kids are older, that I had set up better guidelines about how much time they could spend watching TV when they were younger. I think our last child watches too much TV.*

Here are some ways of helping kids become media savvy while protecting them from media's dark side:

Limit TV viewing (and computer usage and video-game playing). During the school year this isn't as difficult. Our children do not have tons of extra time between homework and extracurricular activities. At least once a week we have a "no TV" night, when everyone either plays board or card games, reads, or works on fun projects. If the weather is nice, there's always the popular "Go outside and play." When everyone has more time on their hands in the summer, we institute a Popsicle-stick system for electronic activities. Each child receives a different colored set of six sticks or less. One stick represents thirty minutes of video game, computer, or TV time. When a child spends thirty minutes engaged in one of these activities, he or she places a stick in a plastic cup in the kitchen. Once all the sticks are gone, that's it for the day. Sticks unused on one day are not transferable to the next. This system allows kids to make choices of how they want to spend their time, yet limits their media exposure.

Even if you do restrict the amount of time kids spend on media pursuits, you still aren't released from the responsibility of monitoring what they watch and play. Content is at least as important as quantity. The TV out on our front porch (where the kids usually play) does not have access to any premium channels. You can make monitoring easier by placing TVs, computers, and video-game players in centralized, high-traffic areas of the house instead of in kids' rooms.

Discuss what's on the screen. When you are watching a show with your children, talk about the plot and moral of the story (if there is one). Being exposed to a thought, action, or idea is one thing; understanding it is another. Ask a few pertinent questions to get kids talking and to help them recognize that real-life actions have consequences, even if they don't on TV. For example, children in a movie may get away with stealing something from a store, but theft has serious consequences, not the least of which is the embarrassment of returning the item and making restitution. Stories abound on the evening news of home invasions and abductions. Let kids know that you do everything you can to ensure their safety. Show them how the deadbolts on your doors keep others out, versus the screen doors and open windows of crime victims on the news. In a video game, the hero may seriously injure his opponent, only to come back strong in the next game. However, you can bet there will be serious consequences to trying out a new fighting move on a sibling!

One final comment about keeping kids safe. Some middle-years kids spend time messaging their friends or communicating in chat rooms. Most online services offer filtering software that prevents children from viewing inappropriate Web sites and allows parental controls to block improper contacts. Let your youngsters know that it's dangerous to give out any kind of personal information on the Internet. You may want to post a list of online rules next to the computer to avoid any misunderstandings.

Too much media time is just one example of how a bad habit, taken to the extreme, can evolve into a vice—one we have the power to banish from our lives. I'm not sure if being disorganized actually could develop into a vice, but it certainly can be another bad habit. Just like adults, some children are innately organized while others are natural messies. I have one child who throws toys, books, and school papers into big piles, which he never would clean up if not coerced. Another child likes to have different colored file folders to keep schoolwork neat. This year she also asked for an accordion folder so that her file folders could be organized by subject. However, just because kids are organized in one area of their lives doesn't mean the tendency carries over across the board. The "pile child" is the one who almost always puts his clean clothes away, while the "neat freak" shoves things anywhere that's handy, like the floor of her closet or under the bed.

If your child is disorganized, there is hope. I was terrified at the thought of my son leaving the relatively safe and orderly world of elementary school for the busy and harsh environment of junior high. He had trouble remembering assignments with just one teacher a day. Papers would remain at school in his desk or locker until the end of the year. When he did begin junior high, something wonderful happened. He discovered his own organizational style. My willingness to provide whatever supplies he thought would help, without fear of how I would react if several file folders or notebooks were never used, gave him the freedom to use trial and error until he came up with a system that worked for him.

For more introspective adults, Cindy Glovinsky describes why it's such a struggle to find the perfect organizational system in her book *Making Peace with the Things in Your Life*: "While a new system may make it easier to solve problems with clutter and disorganization, no system alone will resolve the issue: in most cases disorganization and clutter result not from lack of a system but from counterproductive habits. Making peace with Things is mostly a matter of replacing counterproductive habits with constructive ones."[26] In the previous example, my son managed to integrate notebooks, folders, and a little coaching from Mom into new constructive habits of his own.

Organizational skills can be learned, layer by layer. The old saying "A place for everything and everything in its place" was written for those in search of organization. Encourage your child to become invested in being organized by asking for her input on where things should go; then designate a "home" for all belongings. Setting up daily routines also helps everyone be more organized.

The prophet Jeremiah addressed the issue of habits when he wrote, "Can the Ethiopian change his skin or the leopard its spots? Neither can you do good who are accustomed to doing evil" (Jeremiah 13:23). Simple acts of repetition can also make us accustomed to doing things right. One mom states, "As long as my children live under my roof, I insist that they go to church just as they must go to school. When they become adults and move away, they will make up their own minds about what to do. I hope this consistent foundation will help them maintain the habit of church attendance later." Another mom uses humor to convince her daughters to follow good habits. When approaching them about daily piano practice, "I just say, 'Have you practiced your piano yet?' If my girls say no, I say, 'Well, the piano's available!'"

Among the very best of habits, scripture emphasizes consistent praise, prayer, and thanksgiving:

Rejoice in the Lord always. I will say it again: Rejoice! (Philippians 4:4).

Jesus told his disciples a parable to show them that they should always pray and not give up (Luke 18:1).

Sing and make music in your heart to the Lord, always giving thanks to God the Father for everything, in the name of our Lord Jesus Christ (Ephesians 5:19–20).

We can build an attitude of gratitude into a good habit through devotion and discipline. Pray whenever the Spirit moves you. Accompany your favorite praise and worship CD by singing to the Lord, and give Him the glory and thanks for all things—even when you are trapped in the minivan!

Mom's Moments

If you are a habitual e-mail user, don't respond to those annoying and embarrassing unsolicited e-mail messages (also known as spam). As much as you want to let them know you aren't interested in their product, asking to be removed from their files only lets spammers know that your e-mail address is legitimate.

Do you have a habit you would like to change? Maybe you can relate to the words of Psalm 51:3: "I know my transgressions, and my sin is always before me." Bad habits can weigh on you just like sin. Pray for God's strength to make one change this week.

Make a list of your positive habits and post it on the refrigerator door or bathroom mirror. Ask close friends and family members to contribute what they feel you do best. Focus more on what you do right than on things that need improvement, so that these positives will define your character.

Image Isn't Everything

O Lord, you are our Father.
We are the clay, you are the potter;
we are all the work of your hand.

Isaiah 64:8

One of my daughter's favorite sayings is "If everyone jumped off a cliff, would you do it, too?" That's the concept of peer pressure in a nutshell—the pressure to do things you might not normally do because *everyone else* is doing it. When I was in school, we once watched a filmstrip about lemmings. For some unknown reason, during mass migrations, they have a tendency to rush, en masse, over cliffs and drown in the sea. *Not too bright*, I thought, but history is full of instances where groups of people committed unbelievable deeds and reached catastrophic ends, all in the name of belonging. The pressure to fit in begins during the middle years and continues, in varying degrees, for the rest of our lives.

Part of belonging to a group means adopting the trappings of their lifestyle. It's easier to fit in when you have the same stuff as those you enjoy and admire. I still get a guilty twinge when I think about the purchase of our first minivan over eight years ago. (Yes, it's the same one I'm driving now.) Did we buy it more for its practicality, which is undeniable, or because almost every other family with young children had one, too? Where has this "keeping up with the Joneses" mentality gotten us as a society? In 2001, more Americans declared bankruptcy than graduated from college. We worry that our children will define their self-worth by their possessions, as in, "Whoever dies with the most toys wins." What are we teaching our kids about the value of others when we are willing to ruin ourselves financially to be in the right social strata?

In his letter to the Philippians, Paul writes, "Do nothing out of selfish ambition or vain conceit, but in humility consider others better than yourselves. Each of you should look not only to your own interests, but also to the interests of others" (Philippians 2:3–4). Kids can't help but think themselves better than others when we brag about how we've traded up in houses or cars.

One of the first personal instances of peer pressure kids in the middle years experience is a controlling friendship in which one child insists that the other do things his way or "I won't be your friend anymore." The child has a choice: stand up for what he wants to do or go along in the interest of having a playmate. If your youngster comes to you with a similar problem, talk about the difference between true friends and fair-weather friends. Encourage him to seek out friends with similar interests and values. However, not all peer pressure is negative. Friends encouraging your child to try a new positive skill or to stick with a task when he ordinarily would quit exemplify the good in children's relationships.

How do you raise a child who rises above the need to be part of the crowd, whatever the consequences—a child with the confidence to stand up for his beliefs, interests, and values? Teach your kids that it's not always best to be a follower by dumping your own "keeping up with the Joneses" mentality. You set a powerful example for them by *not* having to have the trendiest clothes and a new car in the driveway every couple of years. Here are some helpful tips to equip kids so they won't be as tempted to bow down to peer pressure:

Accept your child for who he is. Provide love, security, and encouragement. Let him know that his personality is unique and valuable. Find ways to boost your child's self-esteem through helping others and with activities that highlight his growing abilities.

Let kids know that diversity is the spice of life. Everyone does not have to be the same. In fact, wouldn't life be boring if they were? Children in the middle years should understand the concept that friends can disagree—it doesn't mean the other person is bad or even wrong.

Tell them that being popular, while tempting, is not as good as being right. Talk about the differences between popularity and friendship. Kids often feel that being popular means you are somebody, while being rejected means you are nobody. True somebodies are the ones who stand firm on their convictions, even if that means making unpopular decisions. "Each one should test his own actions. Then he can take pride in himself, without comparing himself to somebody else, for each one should carry his own load" (Galatians 6:4–5).

Cut down on commercial messages. Today's marketers and advertisers woo children on an unprecedented scale. In our affluent economy, kids spend billions of dollars a year and persuade their parents to spend even more. Corporate America's goal is not only to build brand loyalty but also to create peer rivalry for their goods. Limit your child's exposure to advertising (mainly on TV). Teach her to critique an ad. Is the message saying that buying their product will make you popular?

Encourage them to trust their instincts. Being pressured into doing something they don't want to do likely will end up causing problems or getting them in trouble. Urge them to listen to the voice of God in their heart when it says, "This is wrong."

Slow things down. Kids want more than material things. They still want "old-fashioned" fun, and it's up to us to help them slow down and enjoy life's simple pleasures like going for a bike ride, watching a sunset, or visiting grandparents.

Remind them whose opinion really matters. While it's natural for children to seek acceptance from their peers, reminding them of the importance of other sources of approval never hurts (like their own approval, your approval, and that of our Maker).

In scripture, the story of Shadrach, Meshach, and Abednego provides a powerful example of how the Lord honors those who do right instead of bowing to peer pressure. Daniel (of the lion's den) convinced King Nebuchadnezzar to appoint his three friends, Shadrach, Meshach, and Abednego, as administrators over the province of Babylon. The king became very angry with this trio when they refused to worship a golden image he had erected. Nebuchadnezzar gave them one last chance to be like everyone else and bow before his god or to be thrown into a blazing furnace. The trio replied,

> *"O Nebuchadnezzar, we do not need to defend ourselves before you in this matter. If we are thrown into the blazing furnace, the God we serve is able to save us from it, and he will rescue us from your hand, O king. But even if he does not, we want you to know, O king, that we will not serve your gods or worship the image of gold you have set up" (Daniel 3:16–18).*

The king couldn't ignore such blatant disobedience, so into the furnace went Shadrach, Meshach, and Abednego.

God honored their faithfulness and devotion by saving their lives. When Nebuchadnezzar witnessed the Lord's power, he decreed that no one could say anything against this amazing God, and he gave Shadrach, Meshach, and Abednego promotions. Talk about a reversal of fortune, all because these three friends bucked the system and stood up (literally and figuratively) for their beliefs.

"Their land is full of idols; they bow down to the work of their hands, to what their fingers have made" (Isaiah 2:8). I find it quite amusing that some people will buy anything as long as it is called "designer." We have become a society infatuated with labels; then we are surprised when our elementary-schoolers pester us for an eighty-dollar pair of sneakers. In our house, we have two extremes of label awareness. One child enjoys wearing clothes from a specific store partly because of the admiring comments from friends. Another refuses to wear any designer clothes for fear of being labeled "rich." Consider how we foist our own label consciousness on our children. They spend their early years in GapKids, then graduate to Tommy Hilfiger and Abercrombie & Fitch before they can even read the label. Kids don't care about such things—at first.

Today's advertising firms aim to create brand loyalty at an early age and keep it, along with years of revenues, as children grow. Marketers want youngsters to ask their parents for products by name. They call this influence the "nag factor." Any mom who has had to push a cart through the grocery store while holding on to a child begging for the newest cereal ("five vitamins and minerals and the delicious taste of cookies") understands the power advertising exerts over our children's lives and, by association, our own.

My favorite story about label sensitivity is Hans Christian Andersen's *The Emperor's New Clothes*. In this fairy tale, two swindlers come to town and convince everyone, including the vain emperor, that they can make a suit out of the finest cloth *to be imagined*. Their "hook" (as today's advertisers call it) was that clothes made from their material were invisible to any man who was unfit for his office or was hopelessly stupid. Of course, the emperor paid the swindlers' exorbitant price in advance. Then he and his ministers were too afraid of being considered unfit or stupid to admit that they couldn't see the nonexistent clothes, even as the emperor paraded down the main street of town in his birthday suit.

"When pride comes, then comes disgrace, but with humility comes wisdom" (Proverbs 11:2). I don't have a garment habit that brings disgrace, but I do enjoy new clothes as much as the next woman. (My husband might say that my shoe fetish borders on disgraceful.) Most moms can't afford to clothe themselves and their families strictly in designer clothing. As quickly as kids outgrow their clothes, pricey brands probably would not be the best use of your resources anyway. That doesn't mean we shouldn't empathize with a child's desire to be part of the group by the clothes she wears. There's nothing wrong with splurging on a couple of expensive items, if you have money available. Let your child pick one or two popular items, and go to a discount store for the rest. Another way to handle label sensitivity is to offer to give your child the amount you feel is acceptable to pay for, say, a pair of tennis shoes and have her save to pay the difference for a more expensive pair.

Another image-awareness concern emerges toward the end of the middle years: body image. There is an amazing amount of diversity in the onset and progression of puberty, with girls usually leading the way. If you're thinking fourth or fifth grade is too early to discuss the monthly female cycle with your daughter, think again. The daughter of one of my close friends started her periods in fifth grade. My daughter always seemed to bring up the subject at the most difficult times, like when we were in a long line at Wal-Mart:

Shelby: Mom, what are those things you're buying?

Me: They're something to. . .help Mom stay fresh, honey.

Shelby: Why would you need something to stay fresh?

Me: Can we talk about this later?

Finally, I broached the subject during a one-on-one walk on a camping trip. "Hon, you know how you're always asking me about these things I brought with me—feminine hygiene products?" "Yes." "Well, I'd like to explain why women need them. You know how my body is different from your body?" "No." Obviously this was going to be more difficult than I thought! It was such a relief to find out that I didn't have to go through *everything* at one time, because my daughter wasn't yet ready for the entire "birds and bees" saga. In fact, sex and the reproductive cycle are topics best addressed in small snippets over time. Too much detail too soon can only confuse your child's understanding of the facts.

Youngsters already may be familiar with some reproductive

information if they've experienced the arrival of a younger sibling at home, but honestly, most of us, including me, are squeamish about discussing the *S* word. At the same time, I want to be the one who presents the information to my children so that they get the straight scoop about sex, not just from me but from God. Several Christian publishers have developed series of books that provide spiritual foundations for understanding sexuality, as well as good starting points for age-appropriate talks with your child. (We used the God's Design for Sex series published by NavPress.)

Here is a general list of the things kids should know before reaching adolescence:

- accurate names for parts of the body

- the reproductive cycle, including the contributions of both men and women

- how bodies change during puberty

- the basic nature of sex between husband and wife

- possible consequences of having sex, including pregnancy and disease

Why is it important to discuss matters of sexuality with your child before junior high school? The initial information kids receive about any topic usually makes a big impression. You can avoid having to correct misconceptions and overcome negative feelings by having your say first.

By starting early, you also can avoid a mistake I made in talking about sex with my daughter. I waited too long to broach the subject. By the time we sat down for our "talk" at the end of fifth grade, my daughter was too mortified about the whole subject for us to have a meaningful conversation. I basically had to force her to sit down so I could even explain why I thought the topic needed to be addressed! Making these discussions a natural part of life in the middle years may not eliminate everyone's discomfort, but it will help kids feel less inhibited about sharing their thoughts and questions. Being honest about your nervousness, especially if you explain that this is due to your own upbringing, lets kids know that the subject of sex is legitimate even if you don't say everything just right.

Over two thousand years ago, Aristotle said, "Happiness is self-contentedness." Perhaps the best way to show children that image isn't everything is by demonstrating our self-contentedness with the potter's creation. We are all the work of the Lord's hand, and He doesn't make mistakes. When you think of yourself as a child of God, there's always something wonderful and unique to celebrate.

Mom's Moments

Make it a family project to see how much money you can save the next time you go to buy back-to-school clothes. Donate the savings to a worthy cause chosen by family members.

If you often feel the pull of peer pressure, consider what you are afraid of. Being unpopular? Being alone? Write positive affirmations on index cards and place them around the house to help you feel better about yourself.

If your childhood family never provided the basis for a healthy self-image, ask close friends to contribute one or two things they appreciate about you.

Afterword

For a while they exist as a changeling—a confused and confusing hybrid between a child and the soon-to-be alien creature. Then they morph into the completely alien *teenager*, an irrational (to adults) cave dweller, for their rooms often resemble a dimly lit, debris-strewn cavern. (The phrase *lost in a black hole* actually describes an item misplaced in a teenager's room, not an astronomical phenomenon.)

Even their speech is strange. I'll never forget the time I overheard my son say "dude" to a friend—not once, not twice, but three times in a row. He *never* uses that kind of vocabulary at home. Then there was the time my daughter explained another girl's personality by telling me, "She thinks she's all that." My daughter watched me carefully to see if I could decipher this coded message. Much to her surprise, I responded with, "Oh, so she's a bit conceited?" (See kids, I *do* listen!)

I am now living with *two* bona fide teenagers, an

experience that qualifies me for, in the words of my oldest son, "free sessions with any psychiatrist." In our interactions, I never know if I'll be talking to a person who feels that I'm a constant embarrassment or the child who refuses to go to bed before receiving a hug and a kiss. My "big kids" want to go to the movies and the mall by themselves, and there's talk of. . .driving. This from the child who still rides his bicycle out in front of oncoming traffic. I know it won't be long and they will be taking turns in the minivan. (Does anyone *know* a good psychiatrist?) The reality that my kids are growing up is inescapable now that my son is taller than I am and my daughter and I share a shoe size. I'll need plenty of help to navigate the curves in the road ahead, but the Lord will be there to make the crooked roads straight and the rough ways smooth (Luke 3:5). Just watch out for those speed bumps!

I lift up my eyes to the hills—
where does my help come from?
My help comes from the LORD,
the Maker of heaven and earth. . . .
The LORD will keep you from all harm—
he will watch over your life;
the LORD will watch over your coming and going
both now and forevermore (Psalm 121:1–2, 7–8).

Notes

1. Dorothy Corkille Briggs, *Your Child's Self-Esteem* (New York: Doubleday, 1970), 149.
2. Howard Gardner, *Frames of Mind: The Theory of Multiple Intelligences* (New York: Perseus Books Group, 1983).
3. Mary Leonhardt, *99 Ways to Get Your Kids to Do Their Homework (and Not Hate It)* (New York: Three Rivers Press, 2000), 40–41.
4. Cheri Fuller, *Helping Your Child Succeed in Public School* (Colorado Springs, CO: Focus on the Family Publishing, 1993), 171.
5. Zick Rubin, *Children's Friendships* (Cambridge, MA: Harvard University Press, 1980), 12.
6. Ibid., 94.
7. Gale Berkowitz, "UCLA Study on Friendship among Women," http://www.postpartum.net/friendship.html.
8. Brenda Hunter, *In the Company of Women* (Sisters, OR: Multnomah Books, 1994), 110.
9. Stanley I. Greenspan, *The Secure Child* (Cambridge, MA: Perseus Publishing, 2002), 91.
10. Thomas W. Phelan, Ph.D., *Self-Esteem Revolutions in Children* (Glen Ellyn, IL: Child Management, Inc., 1996), 43–44.
11. Harry Sheehy, *Raising a Team Player* (North Adams, MA: Storey Books, 2002), xxi.
12. Bettie B. Youngs, Ph.D., Ed.D., *Stress and Your Child* (New York: Ballantine Books, 1995), 29.
13. Ibid., 33–34.
14. Beth Wilson Saavedra, *Creating Balance in Your Child's Life* (Chicago: Contemporary Books, 2000), 4.
15. Paul Ekman, *Why Kids Lie* (New York: Penguin Books, 1989), 182–183.
16. Linda and Richard Eyre, *Teaching Your Children Values* (New York: Fireside, 1993), 158.
17. Denis Donovan, M.D., M.Ed., and Deborah McIntyre, M.A., R.N., *What Did I Just Say!?!* (New York: Henry Holt and Company, 1999), 145.
18. Ibid.
19. Hermine Hartley, *Manners Matter* (Uhrichsville, OH: Barbour Publishing, 2002), 57–58, 102, 130, 151–153.
20. Linda Mason, *The Working Mother's Guide to Life* (New York: Three Rivers Press, 2002), 173.
21. Robert Eisenberger, *Blue Monday* (New York, NY: Paragon House, 1989), ix.

22. Judith Wallerstein and Sandra Blakeslee, *What about the Kids?* (New York, NY: Hyperion, 2003), 134–138.
23. Ron L. Deal, *The Smart Stepfamily* (Minneapolis: Bethany House, 2002), 70–71.
24. Elisa Morgan, "Habits," *MOMSense* (January/February 2003), 3.
25. Michael Medved and Diane Medved, Ph.D., *Saving Childhood* (New York: Harper Collins Publishers, 1998), 18.
26. Cindy Glovinsky, M.S.W., A.C.S.W., *Making Peace with the Things in Your Life* (New York: St. Martin's Press, 2002), 19.

About the Author

Cynthia Sumner's gentle humor and practical insights speak to the needs of mothers today. She was the contributing editor of the *MOMSense* magazine, published by MOPS International, for eight years and is the author of four other books—*Timeout for Mom. . .Ahhh Moments*; *Planes, Trains, and Automobiles. . .with Kids!*; *Mommy's Locked in the Bathroom*; and *Family Vacations Made Simple*. Cynthia also is a founding member of the MOPS Speakers' Bureau. She and her husband, John, live in rural Illinois with their three children, Spencer, Shelby, and Ross.

For information about speaking engagements, contact:

Speak Up Speaker Services
1614 Edison Shores Place
Port Huron, MI 48060
Phone: (888) 870-7719
e-mail: speakupinc@aol.com

Visit Cynthia's Web site at:
www.cynthiasumner.com

MOMMY'S LOCKED in the BATHROOM

BY CYNTHIA SUMNER

ISBN 1-58660-979-3
192 pages

Mommy's Locked in the Bathroom is a humorous and practical guide to surviving the stresses of motherhood. Author Cynthia Sumner shows new mothers how they can use this time in their life to grow spiritually and personally, by offering light-hearted yet profound insights from a mother who also experienced the shock of it all when motherhood was more than she expected.

AVAILABLE WHEREVER CHRISTIAN BOOKS ARE SOLD.